STUDY NOTES

SSC

English Language

TABLE OF CONTENT

SR.NO.	TOPIC	PAGE. NO.
1	Idioms and phrases	02 – 20
2	Spotting error	21 – 41
3	Antonym and synonym	42 – 58
4	Narration	59 - 79
5	Sentence improvement	80 – 109
6	One word substitution	110 – 135
7	Fill in the blanks	136 – 153
8	Spellings	154 – 175
9	Voice	176 – 209
10	Cloze test	210 – 231

IDIOMS AND PHRASES

Idioms and phrases are expressions or figures of speech that have a meaning that is different from the literal meaning of the words used. They are often used in everyday conversation and in writing to add color, imagery, and emphasis to language.

Idioms can be difficult to understand for people who are not familiar with the language, culture, and context in which they are used. For example, the idiom "break a leg" is often used to wish someone good luck, but its literal meaning has nothing to do with breaking bones. Similarly, the phrase "spill the beans" means to reveal secret or confidential information but has nothing to do with actual beans or spilling.

Phrases are groups of words that function as a unit within a sentence. They often convey a specific meaning, but may not have the same figurative quality as idioms. For example, the phrase "in a nutshell" means to summarize something briefly, but it is not an idiom because its meaning can be inferred from the words themselves.

Types of Idioms and Phrases

Metaphor: A metaphor is a figure of speech that compares two things that are not alike, in order to convey a figurative meaning. Idioms often use metaphors to create their figurative meanings.

Translation: Translating idioms and expressions between languages can be difficult, as the figurative meaning may not have a direct equivalent in the target language. This can lead to problems in cross-cultural communication and understanding.

Literal Idioms: These are idioms that have a literal meaning that is the same as the meaning of the individual words used. For example, "kick the bucket" is a literal idiom that means to literally kick a bucket.

Figurative Idioms: These are idioms that have a figurative meaning that is different from the literal meaning of the words used. For example, "kick the bucket" is also a figurative idiom that means to die.

Colloquial Phrases: These are phrases that are commonly used in everyday conversation, but may not be understood by people who are not familiar with the culture or language. For example, "hang out" is a colloquial phrase that means to spend time together.

Proverbs: These are phrases that express a general truth or advice. For example, "a stitch in time saves nine" is a proverb that means it's better to address a problem early before it becomes bigger.

Slang: These are informal expressions that are often used in casual or social contexts. For example, "chill out" is a slang phrase that means to relax.

Clichés: These are overused expressions that have lost their original impact or meaning. For example, "time flies" is a cliché that means time passes quickly.

Jargon: These are phrases that are specific to a particular field or industry and may not be understood by people outside of that field. For example, "bandwidth" is a term used in the technology industry to refer to the amount of data that can be transmitted over a network.

Fundamentals of Idioms and Phrases

Figurative meaning: Idioms and phrases have a figurative meaning that is different from the literal meaning of the words used. It's important to understand the figurative meaning in order to use them correctly.

Cultural context: Idioms and phrases are often tied to a specific culture and may not be understood by people outside of that culture. Understanding the cultural context in which they are used is important to avoid misunderstandings.

Common usage: Idioms and phrases are commonly used in everyday conversation and in writing. It's important to be familiar with common idioms and phrases to communicate effectively.

Collocation: Idioms and phrases often have specific words that collocate with them. It's important to use the correct words to convey the intended meaning.

Register: Idioms and phrases can be formal or informal, and using the correct register is important to communicate appropriately in different situations.

Literal meaning: Some idioms and phrases have a literal meaning that is the same as the meaning of the individual words used. Understanding the literal meaning can help in interpreting the figurative meaning.

Usage in context: It's important to use idioms and phrases appropriately in context to avoid confusion or miscommunication.

Examples of Idioms and Phrases

A piece of cake - means something is easy.

Keep your chin up - means to stay positive in a difficult situation

Bite the bullet - means to endure a difficult or unpleasant situation.

It's raining cats and dogs - means it's raining heavily.

Cut to the chase - means to get to the point.

Importance of Idioms and Phrases

Expressiveness: Idioms and phrases can make language more colorful, expressive, and interesting. They add personality and character to language use and can help to convey meaning in a more memorable and impactful way.

Cultural Understanding: Idioms and phrases are often tied to a specific culture, and understanding them can help in understanding the cultural context in which they are used. They can provide insights into the values, beliefs, and customs of a culture, and can help to bridge cultural divides by facilitating cross-cultural communication.

Efficiency: Idioms and phrases can be more efficient than using multiple words to convey a concept or idea. They can help to communicate complex ideas or emotions succinctly, and can save time and effort in language use.

Humor: Idioms and phrases can also be used for humor, by creating unexpected or humorous comparisons or associations. They can make language use more engaging and enjoyable.

Literary and Artistic Value: Idioms and phrases have been used in literature and art for centuries. They can add depth, richness, and complexity to literary works, and can contribute to the artistic and aesthetic value of creative expression.

The Most Common Idioms

Idiom	Meaning	Usage
A blessing in disguise	a good thing that seemed bad at first	as part of a sentence
A dime a dozen	Something common	as part of a sentence
Beat around the bush	Avoid saying what you mean, usually because it is uncomfortable	as part of a sentence
Better late than never	Better to arrive late than not to come at all	by itself
Bite the bullet	To get something over with because it is inevitable	as part of a sentence
Break a leg	Good luck	by itself
Call it a day	Stop working on something	as part of a sentence
Cut somebody some slack	Don't be so critical	as part of a sentence
Cutting corners	Doing something poorly in order to save time or money	as part of a sentence
Easy does it	Slow down	by itself
Get out of hand	Get out of control	as part of a sentence
Get something out of your system	Do the thing you've been wanting to do so you can move on	as part of a sentence

Get your act together	Work better or leave	by itself
Give someone the benefit of the doubt	Trust what someone says	as part of a sentence
Go back to the drawing board	Start over	as part of a sentence
Hang in there	Don't give up	by itself
Hit the sack	Go to sleep	as part of a sentence
It's not rocket science	It's not complicated	by itself
Let someone off the hook	To not hold someone responsible for something	as part of a sentence
Make a long story short	Tell something briefly	as part of a sentence
Miss the boat	It's too late	as part of a sentence
No pain, no gain	You have to work for what you want	by itself
On the ball	Doing a good job	as part of a sentence
Pull someone's leg	To joke with someone	as part of a sentence
Pull yourself together	Calm down	by itself
So far so good	Things are going well so far	by itself
Speak of the devil	The person we were just talking about showed up!	by itself
That's the last straw	My patience has run out	by itself
The best of both worlds	An ideal situation	as part of a sentence
Time flies when you're having fun	You don't notice how long something lasts when it's fun	by itself
To get bent out of shape	To get upset	as part of a sentence

To make matters worse	Make a problem worse	as part of a sentence
Under the weather	Sick	as part of a sentence
We'll cross that bridge when we come to it	Let's not talk about that problem right now	by itself
Wrap your head around something	Understand something complicated	as part of a sentence
You can say that again	That's true, I agree	by itself
Your guess is as good as mine	I have no idea	by itself

Common English Idioms & Expressions

These English idioms are used quite regularly in the United States. You may not hear them every day, but they will be very familiar to any native English speaker. You can be confident using any of them when the context is appropriate.

Idiom	Meaning	Usage
A bird in the hand is worth two in the bush	What you have is worth more than what you might have later	by itself
A penny for your thoughts	Tell me what you're thinking	by itself
A penny saved is a penny earned	Money you save today you can spend later	by itself
A perfect storm	the worst possible situation	as part of a sentence
A picture is worth 1000 words	Better to show than tell	by itself
Actions speak louder than words	Believe what people do and not what they say	by itself
Add insult to injury	To make a bad situation worse	as part of a sentence
Barking up the wrong tree	To be mistaken, to be looking for solutions in the wrong place	as part of a sentence
Birds of a feather flock together	People who are alike are often friends (usually used negatively)	by itself

Bite off more than you can chew	Take on a project that you cannot finish	as part of a sentence
Break the ice	Make people feel more comfortable	as part of a sentence
By the skin of your teeth	Just barely	as part of a sentence
Comparing apples to oranges	Comparing two things that cannot be compared	as part of a sentence
Costs an arm and a leg	Very expensive	as part of a sentence
Do something at the drop of a hat	Do something without having planned beforehand	as part of a sentence
Do unto others as you would have them do unto you	Treat people fairly. Also known as "The Golden Rule"	by itself
Don't count your chickens before they hatch	Don't count on something good happening until it's happened.	by itself
Don't cry over spilt milk	There's no reason to complain about something that can't be fixed	by itself
Don't give up your day job	You're not very good at this	by itself
Don't put all your eggs in one basket	What you're doing is too risky	by itself
Every cloud has a silver lining	Good things come after bad things	by itself
Get a taste of your own medicine	Get treated the way you've been treating others (negative)	as part of a sentence
Give someone the cold shoulder	Ignore someone	as part of a sentence
Go on a wild goose chase	To do something pointless	as part of a sentence
Good things come to those who wait	Be patient	by itself
He has bigger fish to fry	He has bigger things to take care of than what we are talking about now	by itself
He's a chip off the old block	The son is like the father	by itself
Hit the nail on the head	Get something exactly right	by itself
Ignorance is bliss	You're better off not knowing	by itself

It ain't over till the fat lady sings	This isn't over yet	by itself
It takes one to know one	You're just as bad as I am	by itself
It's a piece of cake	It's easy	by itself
It's raining cats and dogs	It's raining hard	by itself
Kill two birds with one stone	Get two things done with a single action	by itself
Let the cat out of the bag	Give away a secret	as part of a sentence
Live and learn	I made a mistake	by itself
Look before you leap	Take only calculated risks	by itself
On thin ice	On probation. If you make another mistake, there will be trouble.	as part of a sentence
Once in a blue moon	Rarely	as part of a sentence
Play devil's advocate	To argue the opposite, just for the sake of argument	as part of a sentence
Put something on ice	Put a project on hold	as part of a sentence
Rain on someone's parade	To spoil something	as part of a sentence
Saving for a rainy day	Saving money for later	as part of a sentence
Slow and steady wins the race	Reliability is more important than speed	by itself
Spill the beans	Give away a secret	as part of a sentence
Take a rain check	Postpone a plan	as part of a sentence
Take it with a grain of salt	Don’t take it too seriously	as part of a sentence
The ball is in your court	It's your decision	by itself
The best thing since sliced bread	A really good invention	as part of a sentence

The devil is in the details	It looks good from a distance, but when you look closer, there are problems	by itself
The early bird gets the worm	The first people who arrive will get the best stuff	by itself
The elephant in the room	The big issue, the problem people are avoiding	as part of a sentence
The whole nine yards	Everything, all the way.	as part of a sentence
There are other fish in the sea	It's ok to miss this opportunity. Others will arise.	by itself
There's a method to his madness	He seems crazy but actually he's clever	by itself
There's no such thing as a free lunch	Nothing is entirely free	by itself
Throw caution to the wind	Take a risk	as part of a sentence
You can't have your cake and eat it too	You can't have everything	by itself
You can't judge a book by its cover	This person or thing may look bad, but it's good inside	by itself

MULTIPLE CHOICE QUESTION

Direction (1-15): Choose the correct meaning of idioms given in the bold point in the sentences.

1. I am sure they will fight **tooth and nail** for their rights.
A. With all their might
B. Without any other weapon
C. Resorting to violence
D. Very cowardly

Answer: A.
Explanation:
tooth and nail: engage in fight using all resources or with all their might.

2. We were in a hurry. The road being zigzag we had to **cut off a corner** to reach in time.
A. To cut a portion of the road.
B. To take a short cut.
C. To go fast.
D. To take an alternative route.

Answer: B
Explanation:
cut off a corner: to do something in the easiest, cheapest, or fastest way or to take a short cut.

3. Discipline is **on the wane** in schools and colleges these days.
A. Declining
B. Increasing
C. Spreading
D. Spiraling

Answer: A
Explanation:
on the wane: to decrease gradually in size, number, strength, or intensity.

4. In spite of the efforts of all peace-loving people, world peace is still a **far cry.**

A. An impracticable idea

B. An abstract idea

C. Out of reach

D. A long way off

Answer: D

Explanation:

far cry: a long way.

5. I felt that it was a **tall order** to expect Monisha to go home alone at twelve in the night.

A. Difficult

B. Too much

C. Customary

D. Simple

Answer: A

Explanation:

tall order: task or job that is difficult to carry out.

6. I cannot get along with a man who **plays fast and loose.**

A. Behaves in an unreliable and insincere way.

B. Has a loose tongue.

C. Lives a life of ease and luxury.

D. Does not know how to behave himself.

Answer: A

Explanation:

plays fast and loses: to behave in a careless manner.

7. There is **no love lost** between two neighbours.

A. Close friendship

B. Cool indifference

C. Intense dislike

D. A love hates relationship.

Answer: C

Explanation:

no love lost: dislike, ill will, hate.

8. The question of abolition of private property is still **a moot point.**

A. Undecided

B. Uncertain

C. Unknown

D. Not clear

Answer: A

Explanation:

a moot point: an issue opens to argument; also, an irrelevant question, a matter of no importance.

9. This regular absenteeism is **bad business** since no work is being completed**.**

A. Bad for business

B. Non-business like

C. An unfortunate event

D. Creating ill-will.

Answer: C

Explanation:

bad business: irresponsible business.

10. When he tells stories about himself, he is inclined to **draw the longbow.**

A. Understates

B. Gets emotional

C. Exaggerates

D. Gets excited

Answer: C

Explanation:

draw the longbow: to exaggerates in telling stories; overstate something.

11. The detective **left no stone unturned** to trace the culprit.

A. Took no pains.

B. Did very irrelevant things

C. Resorted to illegitimate practices.
D. Used all available means.

Answer: D
Explanation:
left no stone unturned: try every possible course of action in order to achieve something.

12. The authorities **took him to task** for his negligence.
A. Gave him additional work.
B. Suspended his assignment.
C. Reprimanded him.
D. Forced him to resign.

Answer: C
Explanation:
took him to task: to criticize someone.

13. In spite of the immense pressure exerted by the militants, the Government has decided not to **give in.**
A. Accedes.
B. Yield
C. Obliges.
D. Confirm.

Answer: B
Explanation:
give in: to finally agree to what someone wants, after refusing for a period of time.

14. Their business is now **on its last legs.**
A. About to fructify.
B. About to perish.
C. About to produce results.
D. About to take off.

Answer: B
Explanation:
on its last legs: near the end of life, usefulness, or existence or about to perish.

15. He **went back on** his promise to vote for me.

A. Withdrew.

B. Forgot.

C. Reinforced.

D. Supported.

Answer: A

Explanation:

Went back on: to failing to keep a promise, or to change a decision or agreement or Withdrew.

Direction (16-24): Choose the correct meaning of the given idioms.

16. To hit the jackpot

A. To gamble

B. To make money unexpectedly.

C. To inherit money.

D. To become bankrupt

Answer: B

Explanation:

To hit the jackpot: have great or unexpected success, especially in making a lot of money quickly.

17. To be up and doing

A. To recover from illness

B. To be actively engaged

C. To progress satisfactorily.

D. To be expressive and explicit.

Answer: B

Explanation:

To be up and doing: active; busy.

18. To read between the lines

A. To concentrate.

B. To read carefully.

C. To suspect.

D. To grasp the hidden meaning

Answer: D
Explanation:
To read between the lines: look for or discover a meaning that is implied rather than explicitly stated.

19. To turn the tables
A. To defeat
B. To oppose
C. To create chaos
D. To change completely the position of disadvantage.

Answer: D
Explanation:
To turn the tables: reverse one's position relative to someone else, especially by turning a position of disadvantage into one of advantage.

20. To put the cart before the horse
A. To offer a person what he cannot eat
B. To force a person to do something
C. To raise obstacles
D. To reverse the natural order of things

Answer: D
Explanation:
To put the cart before the horse: to suggest something is done contrary to a conventional or culturally expected order or relationship.

21. To show the white feather
A. To show signs of cowardice
B. To seek peace
C. To show arrogance
D. To become polite
Answer: A

Explanation:

To show the white feather: a symbol of cowardice.

22. A sop to Cerberus

A. Bribery

B. Hush money

C. Ransom to an enemy

D. Money for compensation

Answer: C

Explanation:

A sop to Cerberus: a concession or bribe to conciliate a person otherwise liable to be troublesome or ransom to an enemy.

23. To look down one's nose at

A. To backbite

B. To show anger

C. To insult in the presence of others

D. To regard with half-hidden displeasure or contempt

Answer: D

Explanation:

To look down one's nose at: to think of or treat (someone or something) as unimportant or not worthy of respect.

24. To cut the cackle

A. To humiliate

B. To annoy someone

C. To act in a friendly way

D. To stop talking and start

Answer: D

Explanation:

To cut the cackle: To stop talking in order to do something more important.

Direction (25-40): Choose the correct meaning of idioms given in bold part in the sentences.

25. He **rides the high horse** because of his high connection.

A. Is famous

B. Talks flatteringly

C. Puts on airs

D. Is prosperous

Answer: C

Explanation:

rides the high horse: To feel proud or puts on airs

26. We should **give a wide berth** to bad characters.

A. keep away from

B. publicly condemn.

C. give publicly to

D. does not sympathise with

Answer: A

Explanation:

give a wide berth: to keep a reasonable distance from someone or something.

27. He **threw cold water** over the project that the secretary had prepared.

A. Encouraged

B. Discouraged

C. Cleared

D. Rejected

Answer: B

Explanation:

threw cold water over: To discourage or deter someone from doing something.

28. I won't mind even if he goes to dogs.

A. Goes mad

B. Is insulted

C. Is ruined

D. Becomes brutal

Answer: C

Explanation:

goes to dogs: to become much worse in quality or character or is ruined.

29. Mr. Roy is known as a **shoplifter** in the city commercial centre.

A. Daily visitor

B. Buyer of all new things

C. Smuggler

D. A thief in guise of customer

Answer: D

Explanation:

shoplifter: a person who takes goods illegally from a shop without paying for them or A thief in guise of customer.

30. Shweta might **scream blue murder**, but I feel Ritu should get the promotion since she is better qualified for the job.

A. Suffer from persecution complex.

B. Try to prove herself as more suited to the job.

C. Regard it as an act of partiality

D. Make a great deal of noise and object vehemently.

Answer: D

Explanation:

scream blue murder: make an extravagant and noisy protest.

31. Whenever I meet him, he **pulls a long face**.

A. Looks angry.

B. Looks cheerful.

C. Looks gloomy.

D. Looks indifferent.

Answer: C

Explanation:

pulls a long face: to look sad, glum, disapproving.

32. The parliamentary inquiry into the before deal has not **brought to light** any startling facts.

A. Proved
B. Highlighted
C. Disclosed
D. Probed

Answer: C
Explanation:
brought to light: made known or Disclosed

33. He is a plain, simple, and sincere man. He will always **call a spade a spade.**
A. say something to be taken seriously
B. desist from making controversial statement
C. find meaning or purpose in your action
D. be outspoken in language

Answer: D
Explanation:
call a spade a spade: speak plainly without avoiding unpleasant or embarrassing issues.

34. It is difficult to **keep a level head** in these days of mounting prices.
A. Remain cool and composed
B. Eke out existence
C. Make both ends meet
D. Maintain standard of living

Answer: A
Explanation:
keep a level head: to remain calm.

35. Sumit had to look **high and low** before he could find his scooter key.
A. Nowhere
B. Always
C. Everywhere
D. Somewhere

Answer: C
Explanation:
high and low: To look absolutely everywhere for someone or something.

introduction

"Spotting error" is a term used to describe the process of identifying and correcting mistakes or errors in each piece of writing or code. The purpose of spotting errors is to improve the accuracy, clarity, and overall quality of the written material by identifying and fixing any issues or mistakes that might be present.

The process of spotting errors requires careful attention to detail and a good understanding of the rules and principles that govern the written material. For example, in language learning, a student may need to have a good understanding of grammar and vocabulary to be able to spot errors in a passage of text. In programming, a student may need to have a good understanding of programming concepts and syntax to be able to identify and correct errors in code.

Error Spotting Test is asked in the Verbal Ability Section of General English. The questions asked in the error spotting test have grammatical errors in them. The candidate is supposed to find the errors correctly. Generally, one question has one error. But at times there can be multiple. Despite being simple to understand, it is difficult to tackle this question without practice. However, if with sufficient practice and by using the tips given below, any candidate can ace this section. Spotting Errors in English is one of the important topics.

Why Do Exams Have an English Error Spotting

Words, phrases, and sentences can be called the roots of any language. An error in their usage leaves an incomprehensible expression. It would be difficult to understand such sentences and it may also alter the meaning of the sentence. Hence, we must know the roots of the language so that we can.

understand the written text and its expression perfectly. An Error Spotting Test is to judge a candidate's complete knowledge of parts of speech, and grammar.

Tips To Do Well In English Error Spotting In Exams

Here are some expert tips which will help you ace in the Error Spotting Test.

Know Your Parts of Speech.

Parts of Speech form the basic knowledge of English Grammar. A candidate should be able to identify the parts of speech in a sentence correctly.

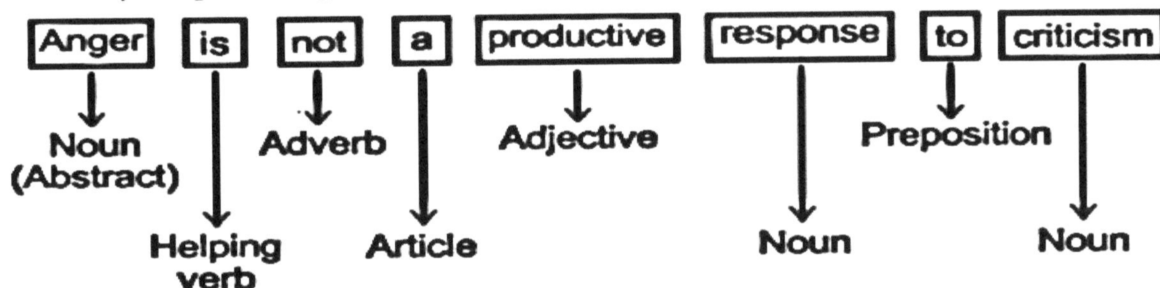

Know Your Sentence Type:

Different types of sentences have different structures. The candidate must identify the sentence to spot the error.

Example

- What is your name. -WRONG
- What is your name? -CORRECT

This is an interrogative sentence. Hence, it must end with a question mark. Similarly, an exclamatory sentence must end with an exclamation mark.

Know Your Punctuation

Punctuation is important for the sentence to make sense. Without the knowledge of punctuation, candidates can miss the errors.

Know The Exceptions

Many rules of grammar have exceptions to them. Make sure you make a careful note of every single exception. Many questions are based on them.

Example

- I will be there in a hour. -WRONG

- I will be there in an hour. -CORRECT

In articles, the words starting with vowel sounds are also preceded with 'An'. Hour is pronounced as 'our'. Hence, it becomes an hour.

Check the Pronoun

A text should always have one type of pronoun in it. If the pronoun changes anywhere in the middle, it is an error.

Example

- One must not tell lies. He must always obey the elders. -WRONG
- One must not tell lies. One must always obey elders. -CORRECT

Here, the text starts with the pronoun 'One' and it should be maintained throughout the text.

Singularity and Plurality

We use certain words to represent the singularity and plurality of nouns. Error questions are based on the use of helping verbs with these words. A candidate must have a thorough understanding of these words.

Example

- The Scissors is missing. -WRONG
- The Scissors are missing. -CORRECT

Here, scissors are one in number. Yet, we use a plural verb with them.

- There is many people in the town. -WRONG
- There are many people in the town-CORRECT.

Here people are a plural term. Hence, we use a plural verb with it.

Questions Tags

A positive statement will have a negative question tag and a negative statement will have a positive question tag. Also, the structure of a question tag is fixed. It starts with a comma after the main sentence, next it has the positive or negative form of the verb, this is followed by the pronoun, and it ends with a question mark.

Example

- You did your homework, didn't you?

A positive statement, negative tag.

- You didn't do your homework, did you?

The negative statement, positive tag.

Traditional Pattern of Error Spotting

In this type of error spotting a sentence is divided into four parts in the question itself, you have to find out which part is correct.

Q) A day after the Delhi government said none of the four convicts in the Nirbhaya(A)/ gang rape and murder case could be hung on the scheduled date of January 2(B)/ as one of them had moved a mercy plea, a Delhi court on Thursday directed(C)/ Tihar jail authorities to submit a report about the status of the scheduled execution (D).

Ans. Part A is grammatically correct, and the remaining parts contain an error. Part (B) gang rape and murder case could be hung on the scheduled date of January 2- is grammatically incorrect because here 'hung' is incorrect as per the context of the sentence, for situations where someone is given death sentence we use 'hanged' not 'hung'. Hang (V1) Hung (V2) Hung (V3) means to attach or place something so that it is held up without support from below. Hang (V1) Hung (V2) Hung (V3) means to die by being suspended by the neck. Part (C) as one of them had moved a mercy plea, a Delhi court on Thursday directed- is grammatically incorrect because present perfect tense will be used instead of past perfect as a point of time is absent and, in such cases, we use the present perfect tense. Hence, 'had' will be replaced with 'has'. Present Perfect: When an action is done in the near past, but we don't know the exact point of time or period, in this situation, the present perfect is used.

- Ravi has submitted his college fees.
- I have had my breakfast.
- Shivani has done her graduation in mass communication.

Part (D) Tihar jail authorities to submit a report about the status of schedule execution. - is grammatically incorrect because we are using past tense in this case as the hearing date is already fixed so past tense will be used. We will replace 'schedule' with 'scheduled'.

The correct sentence will be-

A day after the Delhi government said none of the four convicts in the Nirbhaya gang rape and murder case could be hanged on the scheduled date of January 2 as one of them has moved a mercy plea, a Delhi court on Thursday directed Tihar jail authorities to submit a report about the status of the scheduled execution.

Error spotting rules

Rule 1: Check and identify the part of the speech.

A part of speech classifies the way a word functions in a sentence. There are eight parts of speech in English Grammar: interjection, adjective, pronoun, verb, noun, preposition, adverb, and conjunction. For finding the part of speech of any sentence, check the function and role of words in a sentence.

If the word is a naming word, like having a name of any place, person and so forth, then the sentence is a noun.

If the word is replacing the noun, then it is the pronoun.

If the word is showing an action, then it is the verb.

If the word depicts the quality of a noun, then it is an adjective.

If the word is modifying the verb and adjective, it is an adverb.

If the word connects the other words, then it is a conjunction.

If the word describes the relationship between noun and pronoun, then it is a proposition.

Example:

Q: Ram are playing.

Ans: Here, ram is a noun and "are" is not a correct helping verb. So, correct formation of this sentence is:

Ram is playing.

Rule 2: Identify the type of sentence.

The three kinds of sentences in English Grammar are interrogative, affirmative, and negative sentences. If the sentence is written in the general form, with subject, verb, and object, then, the sentence is affirmative. If the sentence consists of a 'not' with the verb, the sentence is negative. If the helping verb of the sentence is written in the beginning or it consists of question words like why, how, where, then the sentence is interrogative.

Example:

Q: How are you going?
Answer: Where are you going?

Rule 3: Check the punctuation.
Punctuation plays a major role in demonstrating the exact rhythm of the paragraph. Checking commas, question marks, full stops, and other punctuations is important. If two sentences are joined to form one sentence, then they must have a comma in between to show the separation. If the sentence is ending, then it must have a full stop. And, if the sentence consists of a question word and a helping word in the beginning, then it must have a question mark.

Example:

Q: How are you,
Answer: How are you?

Rule 4: Identify the pronouns.
Pronouns are words used in place of nouns. Different types of pronouns take different nouns in the sentences, so one must know the correct pronoun while replacing a noun.
Example:

Q: Ram is a boy. She is playing cricket.
Answer: Ram is a boy. He is playing cricket.

Rule 5: Identify the singularity and plurality.
Sentences in the English language are either singular or plural. There are specific rules to identify which sentence is singular and plural. Typically, the s/es are checked to identify the nouns and sentences as singular or plural.

Example:

Q: Many boy are dancing together.
Answer: Many boys are dancing together.

MULTIPLE CHOICE QUESTIONS

Direction: Identify the part of the sentence that has an error.

1. Rather than go with Amit, he decided to stay at home.

A. With Amit

B. Rather than go

C. He decides

D. To stay at home

Answer: B

Explanation:

The correct sentence is- "Rather than going with Amit, he decided to stay at home."

Let's understand the sentence.

- The incorrect part is Rather than go.
- Here, go will be replaced by going.
- Grammatically and contextually, going should be used.
- Hence, option B is the incorrect answer.

2. Find the part of the given sentence that has an error in it. If there is no error, choose 'No error'.

I told the tailor/(A) to made a new/(B) dress for me. /(C) No error. (D)

A. (A)

B. (B)

C. (C)

D. (D)

Answer: D

Explanation:

To made a new- the error lies in this part only. We use to + V1, (infinitive), here 'made' is used which is V2 so it should be replaced with 'make'.

Direction: Identify the part of the sentence which has an error.

3. The loss of three friends and a job were the price Patel had to pay for his ill-tempered outbursts.

A. The loss of three friends

B. and a job

C. were the price Patel had to pay
D. for his ill-tempered outbursts.

Answer: C
Explanation:
Correct sentence: The loss of three friends and a job was the price Patel had to pay for his ill-tempered outbursts.
In part C of the sentence, the usage of 'were' is incorrect instead, use 'was'. According to grammar, whenever we use the singular subject, we need to use a singular verb for this.
In the given sentence, the subject is 'loss' that is a noun and a singular noun hence we need a singular verb for this that is 'was'. 'Of' is a preposition and 'three friends and a job' are two prepositional objects of this preposition.

4. The following sentence has been split into four segments. Identify the segment that contains a grammatical error.
He is / the more intelligent / and hardworking student / of our class.
A. the more intelligent
B. of our class
C. and hardworking student
D. He is

Answer: A
Explanation:
Correct Sentence: He is the most intelligent and hardworking student of our class.
The given sentence is grammatically incorrect.
Here, 'the most intelligent' should be used instead of 'the more intelligent'.
There are different ways to form the comparative and superlative degrees of adjectives.
Add -er or more to form the comparative of most one-syllable and two-syllable adjectives.

Direction: Find out which part has an error and mark it as your answer. If there is no error, mark 'No error' as your answer.
5. The fans are (A)/enough knowledgeable (B)/to give that understanding (C)/ No error (D)
A. (A)
B. (B)
C. (C)
D. (D)

Answer: B

Explanation:

Correct sentence: The fans are knowledgeable enough to give that understanding.

The error lies in part (B) of the sentence.

- The part 'enough knowledgeable' of the sentence is grammatically incorrect.
- As a grammatical rule, adjectives like 'knowledgeable' should always be placed before 'enough.'
- Structure: Adjective + enough
- Example: She was kind enough to send one of her beautiful dresses.
- Therefore, the use of 'enough knowledgeable' in part '(B)' part of the sentence should be replaced by 'knowledgeable enough' to make it grammatically correct. Hence, the correct answer is '(B).'

Direction: The following sentence has been split into four segments. Identify the segment that contains a grammatical error.

6. Had you / not reached in time, / we will have / lost our lives.

A. Had you

B. lost our lives

C. not reached in time

D. we will have

Answer: D

Explanation:

Correct sentence: Had you not reached in time, we would have lost our lives.

In the given sentence, the use of the simple future tense "will have" is incorrect.

- The given sentence is the third conditional sentence explaining that present circumstances would be different if something different had happened in the past.
- The third conditional sentence format: past perfect, modal auxiliary (would, could, should, etc.) + have + past participle.
- When using the third conditional, we use the past perfect (i.e., had + past participle) in the if-clause and the modal auxiliary (would, could, should, etc.) + have + past participle in the main clause.
- Therefore, the past form of the verb 'would' should be used in place of the simple future form of the verb 'will'.

Direction: The following sentence has been split into four segments. Identify the segment that contains a grammatical error.

7. Rahul sings / very sweet / when he is / in a good mood

A. very sweet

B. when he is

C. in a good mood

D. Rahul sings

Answer: A

Explanation:

Correct Sentence- Rahul sings very sweetly when he is in a good mood.

Here 'sweet' is an adjective which qualifies a subject (Noun/ Pronoun)

However, an 'adverb' is required to modify a Verb

Example- Phillip sings loudly in the shower.

Thus, 'sweet' will be replaced by 'sweetly'.

Direction: In the following question, some part of the sentence may have errors. Find out which part of the sentence has an error and select the appropriate option. If a sentence is free from error, select 'No Error'.

8. I was shocked (A)/ to see how much my grandmother had aged (B)/ since the last time we visited her. (C)/ No Error (D)

A. A

B. B

C. C

D. D

Answer: D

Explanation:

The given sentence has no errors.

The sentence is in the past tense, so we use the past tense form of the verbs i.e., shocked, and aged. **'Since'** has been used to refer to a point of time in the past.

Direction: Select the segment of the sentence that contains a grammatical error. If there is no error, mark 'No error'.

9. Each of the survivors of the Tsunami have been offered free psychological consultation to ease the trauma, by some of the top consultants.

A. No error
B. Each of the survivors of the Tsunami have been offered.
C. trauma, by some of the top consultants
D. free psychological consultation to ease the

Answer: B

Explanation:

We need to change 'have' into 'has' because 'each' is always followed by the singular verb.
Each of the + plural noun + singular verb.
Thus, the correct sentence is: Each of the survivors of the Tsunami has been offered free psychological consultation to ease the trauma, by some of the top consultants.

Direction: In the following questions, one part of the sentence may have an error. Find out which part of the sentence has an error.

10. Encouraging healthy competition(P)/ between the students of the school(Q)/ was one of the objectives of the annual sports day(R)/ No error (S).
A. P
B. Q
C. R
D. S

Answer: B

Explanation:

Correct sentence: Encouraging healthy competition among the students of the school was one of the objectives of the annual sports day.
In the above-given sentence, 'between' will be replaced by 'among'.
'Between' can be used for any number of elements as long as the elements are separate or distinct.

- For Example - Negotiations between the member states collapsed last night.

'Among' is used when talking about people or things that are not distinct and are viewed as a group.

- For Example -There wasn't much unity among the council members.

Here the students are more than two in number (i.e., they represent a group) so the word 'between' will not be used not used and since 'the students' in the given sentence are a part of a class of people so the word 'among' should be used here.

Direction: Identify the segment in the sentence which contains the grammatical error from the given options.

11. The government employees (A)/ went doors to doors in a (B)/ village to fetch some data. (C)/ No error (D)

A. A

B. B

C. C

D. D

Answer: B

Explanation:

Correct sentence: The government employees went door to door in a village to fetch some data.

If a preposition comes after a noun and the same noun gets repeated, the noun will always be in a singular form.

Direction: Spot the error in the following sentence from the options given below. If there is no error, choose option 4.

12. As soon as(A)/ I reach to my house(B)/ I will send you the driver(C)/ No Error(D).

A. A

B. B

C. C

D. D

Answer: B

Explanation:

Correct sentence: As soon as I reach my house, I will send you the driver.

According to the rule, 'reach' is a transitive verb hence after a transitive verb we need to write a direct object.

So, we will remove the preposition 'to' after the verb 'reach'.

Example: They didn't reach the motel until after dark.

Direction: In the following question, some part of the sentence may have errors. Find out which part of the sentence has an error and select the appropriate option. If a sentence is free from error, select No Error.

13. Hundred rupees were (1) the amount (2) she won. (3) No error (4)

A. 1
B. 2
C. 3
D. 4

Answer: A
Explanation:
The incorrect part of the sentence would be part A.
When a plural noun explains a specific amount, the verb should be singular.
The correct replacement should be ‘was. So, the correct sentence would be:
Hundred rupees was the amount she won.

Direction: Find out which part has an error and mark it as your answer. If there is no error, mark ‘No error’ as your answer.
14. Everybody understands that (A)/ Australian continent is reeling under the worst (B)/ forest fires of its history, don't they? (C)/ No error (D).
A. (A)
B. (B)
C. (C)
D. (D)

Answer: D
Explanation:
A short question following a statement is called a question tag. It is used for checking information that we think we know is true.

- The rules for making question tag are:
- The statement and the question tag must be in the same tense.
- If the statement is positive, the question tag must be negative or vice versa.
- Always use a pronoun in the question tag.
- Use the contracted form of "helping verb" and "not" in the negative question tag.
- **Example:** didn't, won't, etc.

Words like everyone, each, every, nobody, no one, anybody, etc., are singular and take all singular parts of speech. However, their question tag will take a plural verb and a plural pronoun.
Hence, in the given sentence, plural form of verb has been used with with plural pronoun 'they' e.g., don't they?

Direction: In the following sentence there may an error. Choose the part of the sentence which has the error.

15. The story of the spirits residing in the building is a myth and will remains so.

A. The story of the spirits residing

B. in the building is a myth

C. and will remains so.

D. No error

Answer: C

Explanation:

The error lies in option C as the verb 'remains' is incorrect and must be replaced with the verb 'remain' as with 'will' we always use the infinitive form of the verb.

The correct form should be: 'and will **remain** so.'

Direction: Each question in this section has a sentence with three parts labelled (A), (B) and (C). Read each sentence to find out whether there is an error in any part and if you find no error, your response should be indicated as (D).

16. No man-made disaster(A)/ can surpass the fury of nature. (B)/ He is the most powerful. (C)/ No error(D)

A. (A)

B. (B)

C. (C)

D. (D)

Answer: C

Explanation:

Nature should take the pronoun 'she' instead of 'he' as nature when personified is usually projected as feminine gender.

Correct sentence: No man-made disaster can surpass the fury of nature. She is the most powerful.

Direction: Identify the part of the sentence that has an error.

17. Once appointed by the President, (A)/the council of ministers (B)/as responsible (C)/to the house. (D)

A. Once appointed by the President

B. the council of ministers

C. as responsible

D. to the house

Answer: C

Explanation:

Change 'are' to 'is' because the subject 'council of ministers' is considered as one unit.

Direction: Identify the part of the sentence that has an error.

18. The time has come for policy makers (A) / in India to understand the damage (B) / which is caused as a result of (C) / a vast gap in perception and reality. (D)

A. The time has come for policy makers

B. in India to understand the damage

C. which is caused as a result of

D. a vast gap in perception and reality

Answer: C

Explanation:

Change 'is' to 'has been' to correct the error of tense to indicate that the damage has been done in present perfect.

Direction: Identify the part of the sentence that has an error.

19. The perception of security (A)/held by the power elites (B)/tend to ignore the basic reality that (C)/contradictions of civil society have grown since nuclear explosion. (D)

A. The perception of security

B. held by the power elites

C. tend to ignore the basic reality that

D. contradictions of civil society have grown since nuclear explosion

Answer: C

Explanation:

Change 'tend' to 'tends' to correct the error of subject verb agreement. Because the subject 'the perception of security' is expressing one or singular idea.

Direction: Identify the part of the sentence that has an error.

20. Since two days, (A)/I have not taken (B)/the breakfast (C)/but dinner. (D)

A. Since two days

B. I have not taken

C. the breakfast

D. but dinner

Answer: C

Explanation:
Delete 'the' before breakfast. Because before 'meal' article is not used except for a particular purpose.

Direction: Identify the part of the sentence that has an error.
21. Any coalition (A)/which contains Miss Jayalalitha as a major ally (B)/and Ms. Mamta as a minor partner (C)/do not need outside support. (D)
A. Any coalition
B. which contains Miss Jayalalitha as a major ally
C. and Ms. Mamta as a minor partner
D. do not need outside support

Answer: D
Explanation:
Change 'do not' to 'does not' to correct the error in subject-verb agreement. Because the subject is 'Any coalition' (singular).

Direction: Identify the part of the sentence that has an error.
22. The bus ride to Lahore (A)/went smoothly (B)/and so did (C)/the cricket match. (D)
A. The bus ride to Lahore
B. went smoothly
C. and so did
D. the cricket match

Answer: B
Explanation:
Use 'went off' to correct the error in phrasal verb. 'went off' means 'taken place in the specified way'.

Direction: Identify the part of the sentence that has an error.
23. Quite a few (A)/students were also present (B)/during farewell ceremony (C)/of their outgoing principal. (D)
A. Quite a few
B. students were also present
C. during farewell ceremony
D. of their outgoing principal

Answer: C
Explanation:

Use article 'the' before 'farewell', because farewell in this sentence is organized for the outgoing principal. So it is particularized in the sentence.

Direction: Identify the part of the sentence that has an error.
24. Today, all students (A)/of my class are (B)/invited to dinner (C)/given to bid farewell to the out-going students. (D)
A. Today, all students
B. of my class are
C. invited to dinner
D. given to bid farewell to the out-going students

Answer: C
Explanation:
Add 'a' before dinner because it is a special dinner hosted on a special occasion. Article is not usually used before a regular meal.

Direction: Identify the part of the sentence that has an error.
25. Only few (A)/customers come (B)/regularly (C)/to my shop. (D)
A. Only few
B. customers come
C. regularly
D. to my shop

Answer: A
Explanation:
Change 'few' to 'a few'. Because 'few' has almost a negative meaning but when 'only' is used before 'few', 'a' is used before 'few' to denote that number is very small but not negative.

Direction: Identify the part of the sentence that has an error.
26. After having failed to revive a flagging Nano, (A) / Tata Motors has demanded afresh last week (B) / that the enviable sops be extended to other car models (C) / it plans to manufacture from Sanand. (D)
A. After having failed to revive a flagging Nano,
B. Tata Motors has demanded afresh last week
C. that the enviable sops be extended to other car models
D. it plans to manufacture from Sanand

Answer: A

Explanation:
In part (A) of the given sentence the use of 'After' before the perfect participle 'having failed' is redundant or needless.

Direction: Identify the part of the sentence that has an error.
27. The government has acknowledged that (A) / economic growth did slow down in 2018-19 (B) / owing to declining in private consumption growth (C) / a tepid increase in fixed investments and muted exports. (D)
A. The government has acknowledged that
B. economic growth did slow down in 2018-19,
C. owing to declining in private consumption growth,
D. a tepid increase in fixed investments and muted exports.

Answer: C
Explanation:
Here verb should not be used in gerund form because it is preceded by infinitive "to". Thus instead of "declining", use of "decline" is preferred.

Direction: Identify the part of the sentence that has an error.
28. This perplexing trend may be attributed to (A) / increasing compliance among businesses amidst (B) / the aggressive push by the (C) / tax authorities to wider the tax base. (D)
A. This perplexing trend may be attributed to
B. increasing compliance among businesses amidst
C. the aggressive push by the
D. tax authorities to wider the tax base.

Answer: D
Explanation:
Here instead of comparative degree of adjective "wide" (wider), verb "widen" is to be used in order to connote that the tax base should be increased or broadened.

Direction: Identify the part of the sentence that has an error.
29. A poorly regulated pharmaceutical (A) / industry mean that antibiotics (B) / are freely available to (C) / those who can afford them. (D)
A. A poorly regulated pharmaceutical
B. industry mean that antibiotics
C. are freely available to
D. those who can afford them.

Answer: B

Explanation:

Fragment B is erroneous as Industry is singular, thus the verb "mean" should be used in singular form i.e. means.

Direction: Identify the part of the sentence that has an error.

30. The stakeholders must appreciate (A) / that the only way to postpone (B) / resistance is though improved (C) / hygiene and vaccinations. (D)

A. (A)

B. (B)

C. (C)

D. (D)

Answer: C

Explanation:

Fragment C is erroneous as it uses "though" instead of "through".

31. Find the error in one of the following fragments/parts.

A. The government has acknowledged that

B. economic growth did slow down in 2018-19,

C. owing to declining in private consumption growth,

D. a tepid increase in fixed investments and muted exports.

Answer: C

Explanation:

Here verb should not be used in gerund form because it is preceded by infinitive "to". Thus instead of "declining", use of "decline" is preferred.

32. Find the error in one of the following fragments/parts.

A. The stakeholders must appreciate

B. that the only way to postpone

C. resistance is though improved

D. hygiene and vaccinations.

Answer: C

Explanation:

Fragment C is erroneous as it uses "though" instead of "through".

Direction: Identify the part of the sentence that has an error.

33. That residents are now given minimum piped water and meagre tanker (A) / supplies totalled a third of the installed capacity of 1,494 million litres a day, (B) / that too mainly from desalination plants, faraway lakes and (C) / farm wells, is proof of the neglect of water governance. (D)

A. That residents are now given minimum piped water and meagre tanker.
B. supplies totalled a third of the installed capacity of 1,494 million litres a day,
C. that too mainly from desalination plants, faraway lakes and
D. farm wells, is proof of the neglect of water governance.

Answer: B
Explanation:
The error is in fragment B. The word form 'totalled' makes this sentence incorrect. The correct form of the word which is to be used here is 'totalling' instead of 'totalled'.

Direction: Identify the part of the sentence that has an error.
34. Many of my cousins beat (A) / around the bushes (B) / quite a bit, especially when they have (C) / to give you bad news. (D)
A. (A)
B. (B)
C. (C)
D. (D)

Answer: B
Explanation:
The correct idiomatic expression is 'beat around the bush' and not 'beat around the bushes'. The error hence is in fragment B.

Direction: Identify the part of the sentence that has an error.
35. The Bombay High Court on Thursday upheld (A) / the constitutional validity of (B) / reservation of the Maratha community (C) / in government jobs and education. (D)
A. The Bombay High Court on Thursday upheld
B. the constitutional validity of
C. reservation of the Maratha community
D. in government jobs and education.

Answer: C
Explanation:
The fragment C of the sentence is erroneous. The word 'reservation' should be followed by the preposition 'for' in order to make the sentence meaningfully correct.

Direction: Identify the part of the sentence that has an error.
36. What the index makes clear is that (A) / governments, both central and state, (B) / needs to spend a lot more on health, (C) / and on sanitation, drinking water supply and air quality. (D)
A. What the index makes clear is that
B. governments, both central and state,
C. needs to spend a lot more on health,
D. and on sanitation, drinking water supply and air quality.

Answer: C
Explanation:
The error is in fragment C. The subject 'governments' is plural and should be qualified by the plural form of the verb 'need'.

Direction: Identify the part of the sentence that has an error.
37. Besides, central banks (A) / they have been aggressive in (B) / buying physical gold to (C) / cushion falling currencies. (D)
A. Besides, central banks
B. they have been aggressive in
C. buying physical gold to
D. cushion falling currencies.

Answer: B
Explanation:
The error is in fragment B. Subject here is 'central banks'. The pronoun 'they' is altering the meaning of the sentence and making it absurd.

Direction: Identify the part of the sentence that has an error.
38. The fact that the (A) / crowds got larger and larger are (B) / a reflection of how social media now (C) / feeds the echo chambers of all digital fans. (D)
A. The fact that the
B. crowds got larger and larger are
C. a reflection of how social media now
D. feeds the echo chambers of all digital fans.

Answer: B
Explanation:
The error is in fragment B. The subject 'fact' is singular. Hence the singular verb 'is' should be used instead of 'are' in order to make the sentence correct.

Antonyms and synonyms are two fundamental concepts in language that relate to the meaning of words.

Synonyms are words that have similar or identical meanings. For example, "big" and "large" are synonyms because they both express the concept of size.

Antonyms, on the other hand, are words that have opposite meanings. For example, "warm" and "cold" are antonyms because they express opposite temperatures.

Knowing synonyms and antonyms can be helpful in many ways. For instance, when you are writing or speaking, you can use synonyms to avoid repeating the same words over and over again, which can make your text more interesting and varied. Antonyms, on the other hand, can help you express contrast or opposition, which can add depth and nuance to your language.

Fundamentals of Antonyms

Antonyms are fundamental to language because they help us express contrasts and opposites, which are essential for effective communication. Antonyms are pairs of words that have opposite meanings, such as "warm" and "cold", "good" and "bad", "big" and "small", and so on.

Using antonyms can help us communicate more precisely and convey complex ideas more effectively. For example, in a sentence like "He is tall, but his brother is short," the use of the antonym "short" helps us understand the contrast between the two brothers' heights.

Moreover, learning antonyms is a crucial part of vocabulary development, as it helps us expand our vocabulary and understand how words relate to each other. For instance, if we know the antonym of a word, we can often guess its meaning from the context.

Fundamentals of Synonyms

Synonyms are fundamental to language because they help us to express the same idea in different ways, making our language more varied, interesting, and expressive. Synonyms are words that have the same or similar meanings. For instance, "happy" and "joyful" are synonyms because they both convey the idea of happiness.

Using synonyms can help us avoid repetition, make our writing or speech more engaging and dynamic, and allow us to express ourselves with greater precision and accuracy. For example, instead of repeating the same word multiple times in a sentence or paragraph, we can use synonyms to convey the same idea in different ways, adding depth and richness to our language.

Learning synonyms is also an essential part of building vocabulary and improving language skills. Knowing synonyms can help us expand our vocabulary and understand the subtle nuances of meaning between different words.

In summary, synonyms are an essential component of language that can help us communicate more effectively, express ourselves with greater clarity, and improve our overall language skills.

Kinds of Antonyms

Gradable antonyms: These are antonyms that have opposite ends of a spectrum, such as "hot" and "cold", "tall" and "short", or "fast" and "slow".

Complementary antonyms: These are antonyms that describe two mutually exclusive options, such as "alive" and "dead", "married" and "single", or "on" and "off".

Relational antonyms: These are antonyms that describe a relationship between two things, such as "parent" and "child", "teacher" and "student", or "borrower" and "lender".

Kinds of Synonyms

Exact synonyms: These are synonyms that have the same meaning, such as "big" and "large", "happy" and "joyful", or "car" and "automobile".

Partial synonyms: These are synonyms that have some similar meanings, but also have some differences in their usage or connotation. For example, "buy" and "purchase", "pretty" and "beautiful", or "talk" and "chat".

Here are some terms related to antonyms and synonyms.

Homonyms: These are words that sound the same but have different meanings, such as "flower" and "flour", or "blue" and "blew". Homonyms are not antonyms or synonyms, but they can still cause confusion in language.

Polysemous words: These are words that have multiple meanings, such as "bank" (which can mean a financial institution, the side of a river, or a place to sit). Polysemous words can have antonyms or synonyms depending on the context.

Hyponyms: These are words that are more specific versions of a more general word, such as "dog" (a hyponym of "animal") or "apple" (a hyponym of "fruit"). Hyponyms can have antonyms or synonyms based on their relationship to the more general word.

Hypernyms: These are words that are more general versions of a more specific word, such as "vehicle" (a hypernym of "car") or "fruit" (a hypernym of "apple"). Hypernyms can have antonyms or synonyms based on their relationship to the more specific word.

Some Factors of Antonyms and Synonyms

Meaning: Antonyms are words with opposite meanings, while synonyms are words with similar meanings. Therefore, the meaning of a word is the primary factor that determines whether it is an antonym or a synonym.

Context: The context in which a word is used can also affect whether it is considered an antonym or a synonym. For example, the word "light" can be used as both an antonym and a synonym, depending on the context. In the context of weight, "light" is an antonym of "heavy," while in the context of brightness, "light" is a synonym of "bright."

Usage: Antonyms are often used to contrast two things or concepts, while synonyms are used to emphasize similarity or to avoid repetition. For example, in the sentence "The room was dark, but outside it was light," the antonyms "dark" and "light" are used to contrast two different conditions. On the other hand, in the sentence "The dog barked loudly," the synonyms "barked" and "loudly" are used for emphasis and to avoid repetition.

Frequency: Some words have many synonyms, while others have few or none. Similarly, some words have many antonyms, while others have none. The frequency of use of a word and its relationship to other words in the language can affect the number and type of synonyms and antonyms that exist for it.

Nuance: Sometimes, even if two words have similar meanings, there may be a subtle difference in meaning or connotation that makes one word more appropriate than the other in a given context. This nuance can affect whether two words are considered synonyms or not. Similarly, some antonyms may have shades of meaning that make them appropriate for certain contexts.

Importance of Antonyms and Synonyms

Clarifying Meaning: Antonyms help to clarify the meaning of a word by providing a contrasting term, while synonyms provide a variety of words with similar meanings. This can help to avoid confusion and ensure that the intended meaning is clear.

Vocabulary Development: Learning antonyms and synonyms can help to expand vocabulary and improve language skills. By understanding the different shades of meaning and nuances associated with words, speakers can express themselves more effectively and precisely.

Enhancing Writing Skills: Antonyms and synonyms can be used to add variety and interest to writing. By using a range of synonyms instead of repeating the same word multiple times, writers can make their writing more engaging and effective.

Improved Comprehension: By understanding the meanings of antonyms and synonyms, readers can better understand texts and interpret them correctly.

Enhancing Critical Thinking: Antonyms and synonyms can be used to promote critical thinking skills. By analyzing the relationships between words and their meanings, speakers and writers can develop a deeper understanding of language and its uses.

MULTIPLE CHOICE QUESTION

DIRECTIONS (1- 22):

In each of the following questions, choose the word opposite (or) ANTONYMS in meaning to the given word as your answer.

1. NOVEL

A. Naughty

B. Novelist

C. Banal

D. Nasty

Answer: C

Explanation:

Banal (Adj.): very ordinary and containing nothing that is interesting or important.

Novel (Adj.): different from anything known before; new; interesting seeming slightly strange.

2. HARMONIOUS

A. Sonorous

B. Discordant

C. Concordant

D. Balanced

Answer: B

Explanation:

Discordant (Adjective): not in agreement

Harmonious (Adjective): friendly; peaceful and without any disagreement.

3. ACCELERATE

A. Delay

B. Quickens

C. Diminishes

D. Descent

Answer: A

Explanation:

Delay (Verb): to make/ do late.

Accelerate (Verb): to happen faster or earlier than expected.

4. BOLD

A. Timid

B. Nervous

C. Coy

D. Fearful

Answer: A

Explanation:

Timid (Adjective):shy and nervous.

Bold (Adjective): brave and confident; not afraid

5. TRAITOR

A. Migrant

B. Member

C. Patriot

D. Officer

Answer: C

Explanation:

Patriot (Noun): a person who loves their country and is ready to defend against an enemy.

Traitor (Noun): a person who gives away secrets about their country; one who betrays; renegade; back-stabber.

6. EXAGGERATE

A. Extravagant

B. Understates

C. Abundance

D. Excerpt

Answer: B

Explanation:

Understate (Verb): to state that something is smaller, less important than it really is.

Exaggerate (Verb): to make something seem larger, better, worse or more important than it really is.

7. ACCUMULATE

A. Disperses

B. Dismisses

C. Below

D. Aware

Answer: A

Explanation:

Disperse (Verb): to spread; scatter; to move apart.

Accumulate (Verb): to gradually increase in number; collect; amass; build up.

8. STERILE

A. Fertile

B. Infertile

C. Dense

D. Barren

Answer: D

Explanation:

The word, 'sterile' is an adjective which means 'totally clean'. It also means 'not able to produce children or young'. The word, 'barren' is an adjective which means 'unproductive/infertile'. As the two words are similar in meaning, option B is correct.

9. CONCILIATION

A. Dispute

B. Irritation

C. Separation

D. Confrontation

Answer: D

Explanation:

Confrontation (Noun): a situation in which there is angry disagreement.

Conciliation (Noun): the act of pacifying; the act of making somebody less angry or more friendly.

10. AMELIORATE

A. Improves

B. Depends

C. Softens
D. Worsens

Answer: D
Explanation:
Worsen (Verb)**:** to make or become worse than it was before.
Ameliorate (Verb)**:** to make something better.

11. GLOOMY
A. Radiant
B. Fragrant
C. Melodious
D. Illusory

Answer: A
Explanation:
Radiant (Adjective): showing great happiness, love, or health; giving a warm bright light.
Gloomy (Adjective): nearly dark or badly lit in a way that makes you feel sad; depressing; sad and without hope.

12. EXONERATE
A. Admits
B. Release
C. Convict
D. Reject

Answer: C
Explanation:
Convict (Verb)**:** to decide and state officially in court that somebody is guilty of a crime.
Exonerate (Verb)**:** to officially state that somebody is not responsible for something that he has been blamed for; acquit.

13. RETAIN
A. Remember
B. Release
C. Unfurl
D. Engage

Answer: B

Explanation:

Release (Verb): to let out; to stop holding.

Retain (Verb): to keep; to preserve; to continue to have/ hold/contain.

14. BLEAK

A. Dull

B. Dark

C. Bright

D. Exposure

Answer: C

Explanation:

While all these words mean "bright of cheer or comfort," bleak suggests chill, dull, and barren characteristics that utterly dishearten.

15. PROMINENT

A. Unknown

B. Eminent

C. Renowned

D. Important

Answer: A

Explanation:

Unknown (Adjective): not known.

Prominent (Adjective): noticeable; distinguished; important or well known.

16. MALICIOUS

A. Malevolent

B. Spiteful

C. Baneful

D. Benign

Answer: D

Explanation:

Benign (Adjective): kind and gentle; not hurting anybody; not dangerous or likely to cause death.

Malicious (Adjective): spiteful; malevolent; having/showing hatred and a desire to harm/hurt

17. INCESSANT

A. Continuous

B. Intermittent

C. Unceasing

D. Constant

Answer: B

Explanation:

Intermittent (Adjective): stopping and starting often over a period of time, but not regularly; sporadic.

Incessant (Adjective): never stopping; constant.

18. WARY

A. Conscientious

B. Daring

C. Thrifty

D. Rash

Answer: D

Explanation:

Rash (Adjective): impulsive; reckless; doing something that may not be sensible without first thinking about the possible results

Wary (Adjective): cautious ; careful while dealing with somebody/something.

19. OVERT

A. Open

B. Complete

C. Hidden

D. Culvert

Answer: C

Explanation:

Hidden (Adjective) : not open ; secret ; concealed

Overt (Adjective) : done in an open way and not secretly ; open

20. FLOOD

A. Drought

B. Dry

C. Cyclone
D. Desert

Answer: A
Explanation:
Drought (Noun): a long period of time when there is little or no rain
Flood (Noun): a large amount of water covering an area that is usually dry.

21. LIBERTY
A. Freedom
B. Liberation
C. Bondage
D. Crowded

Answer: C
Explanation:
Bondage (N): the state of being a slave or prisoner; slavery.
Liberty (N): freedom, liberation.

22. REVOKE
A. Negate
B. Annul
C. Invalidate
D. Implement

Answer: D
Explanation:
Implement (Verb): to make something that has been officially decided to start, to happen or be used; carry out.
Revoke (Verb): to officially cancel something so that it is no longer valid; invalidate.

DIRECTIONS (23-40)
Choose the correct meaning of Synonyms given in Capital sentences.

23. LUXURIANT
A. Luxury loving
B. Lovely
C. Rich

D. Abundant

Answer: D
Explanation:
The word Luxuriant (Adjective) means: growing thickly and strongly; rich in something that is pleasant or beautiful; abundant.

24. CANTANKEROUS
A. Cancerous
B. Fissiparous
C. Quarrelsome
D. Ferocious

Answer: C
Explanation:
The word Cantankerous (Adjective) means bad tempered and always complaining. Hence, the words cantankerous and quarrelsome are synonymous.

25. TRITE
A. Clever
B. Brief
C. Impudent
D. Commonplace

Answer: D
Explanation:
The word Trite (Adjective) means: dull and boring because it has been expressed so many times before; not original; banal; very ordinary and containing nothing that is interesting or important.
Hence, the words trite and commonplace are synonymous.

26. DERISION
A. Condemnation
B. Ridicule
C. Embarrassment
D. Humiliation

Answer: B
Explanation:

The word Derision (Noun) means ridicule; mockery; a strong feeling that somebody/ something is ridiculous and not worth considering seriously.

27. ONUS

A. Sadness

B. Responsibility

C. Happiness

D. Criticism

Answer: B

Explanation:

The word Onus (Noun) means: the responsibility for something.

28. FLIMSY

A. Partisan

B. Weak

C. Irrational

D. Funny

Answer: B

Explanation:

The word Flimsy (Adjective) means badly made and not strong enough: thin and easily torn.

Hence, the words flimsy and weak are synonymous.

29. CODDLE

A. Huddle

B. Satisfy

C. Protect

D. Cheat

Answer: B

Explanation:

The word Coddle (Verb) means: to treat somebody with too much care and attention, pamper, cosset.

Hence, the words coddle and satisfy are synonymous.

30. PROPHYLACTIC

A. Toxic

B. Antagonistic

C. Preventive
D. Purgative

Answer: C
Explanation:
The word Prophylactic means:
The course of action is used to prevent disease.
Hence, the words prophylactic and preventive are synonymous.

31. OSTRACIZE
A. Besiege
B. Beguile
C. Belittle
D. Banish

Answer: D
Explanation:
The word Ostracise (Verb) means: to refuse to let somebody; a member of a social group: refuse, shun.
Hence the words banish and ostracize are synonymous.

32. DEBACLE
A. Decline
B. Degeneration
C. Downfall
D. Discomfiture

Answer: C
Explanation:
The word Debacle (Noun) means:
an event or a situation that is a sudden or complete failure.
Hence, the words debacle and downfall are synonymous.

33. ACCRUE
A. Accumulate
B. Suffice
C. Accommodate
D. Grow

Answer: A

Explanation:

The word Accrue (Verb) means: to increase over a period of time; to allow a sum of money or debts to grow over a period of time.

Therefore, accumulate is the correct nearest word.

34. GENIAL

A. Specific

B. Careful

C. Unselfish

D. Cordial

Answer: D

Explanation:

The word Genial (Adjective) means friendly and cheerful; affable; cordial.

35. INCLEMENT

A. Unfavorable

B. Inactive

C. Selfish

D. Active

Answer: (a)

Explanation:

The word Inclement (Adjective) means not pleasant; unfavorable; cold, wet etc.

36. VINDICTIVE

A. Aggressive

B. Spiteful

C. Accusative

D. Imaginative

Answer: B

Explanation:

The word Vindictive (Adjective) means: trying to harm or upset somebody or showing that you want to, because you think that they have harmed you; spiteful; revengeful.

Spiteful is the correct synonym as it means having or showing a desire to harm, anger, or defeat someone.

37. LOQUACIOUS

A. Slow

B. Talkative

C. Unclear

D. Content

Answer: B

Explanation:

The word Loquacious (Adjective) means talking a lot; talkative is the right synonym while others have different meanings.

38. PERSPICUOUS

A. Clear

B. Brief

C. Precise

D. Relevant

Answer: C

Explanation:

The word Perspicuous (Adjective) means precise clear and accurate.

39. PRODIGAL

A. Carefree

B. Lavish

C. Productive

D. Productive

Answer: B

Explanation:

The word Prodigal (Adjective) means too willing to spend money or waste time, energy, or materials extravagant lavish.

40. INFAMY

A. Familiarity

B. Integrity

C. Glory

D. Notoriety

Answer: D

Explanation:

The word Infamy (Noun) means: the state of being well known for something bad or an evil act notoriety.

NARRATION

Introduction

Narration refers to any type of explanation or telling of something. It is commonly used in the context of storytelling. Narration is often used in literature, film, television, and other forms of media to engage the audience and convey a message or meaning. In written form, narration typically takes the form of a narrative or a story that is told from a specific point of view, such as first-person, second-person, or third person. In spoken form, narration can take the form of a monologue, dialogue, or other types of speech.

Narration, also known as direct and indirect speech, is a fundamental aspect of communication in both written and spoken language. Narration is used to report or retell something that someone has said, either in its original form or rephrased to fit a new context. Narration is an essential tool for writers, journalists, and anyone who wants to accurately report what someone has said. This paper will discuss the different types of narration, including direct and indirect speech, as well as the rules and guidelines for using them correctly.

Types of Narration

The two main types of narration are direct speech and indirect speech. Direct speech is when the exact words of the speaker are quoted and placed inside quotation marks. For example, "I love ice cream," said John. In this example, John's words are quoted directly, and his exact words are placed inside quotation marks. Direct speech is commonly used in fiction writing, news reporting, and interviews.

Indirect speech, on the other hand, is when the speaker's words are retold or reported without being quoted directly. In indirect speech, the speaker's words are rephrased to fit into a new context. For example, John said that he loves ice cream. In this example, John's words are not quoted directly, but his message is conveyed in a different way. Indirect speech is commonly used in news reporting, academic writing, and business communication.

Direct speech

In general, direct speech is a sentence in which the speaker's exact words are used to state what the speaker has said by using his words. Direct speech causes repetition of the exact words spoken or said by the speaker in speech marks or quotation marks.

In other words, we express a speech in direct speech as if the original speaker is speaking for himself. There is no change in the words or the tenses of the verbs. In this case, we use a reporting clause or verb to indicate that we are referring to someone else's speech or words, such as he said, she said, and so on. Then comes the reported clause, which is the speaker's original speech.

Rules for direct speech

There are a few rules to keep in mind when using direct speech. First, the exact words of the speaker should be placed inside quotation marks. Second, a comma should be placed before the opening quotation mark. For example, "I love ice cream," said John. Third, the speech should be attributed to the speaker using a reporting verb such as 'said', 'asked', or 'shouted'. Finally, the first letter of the first word of the speech should be capitalize. For example, "I love ice cream," said John.

Indirect speech

This is a speech or system of narrating a person's speech in which we are not required to use the exact same words as the speaker. Indirect speech is the sentence in which we convey or narrate a speech by rephrasing it in our own words.
No quotation marks are used in indirect speech to quote the speaker's words. Only the speech's most important or necessary parts are reproduced here using different words. The only goal is to convey the same message.

We use a reporting clause similar to a direct speech here, followed by a reported clause. The 'that' clause is the most common way to express words in indirect speech. However, depending on the circumstances, the reported clause may change. If it's a question, for example, use 'if' or 'whether.' 'To' is a command that can be used.

Rules for Using Direct Speech

There are a few rules to keep in mind when using direct speech. First, the exact words of the speaker should be placed inside quotation marks. Second, a comma should be placed before the opening quotation mark. For example, "I love ice cream," said John. Third, the speech should be attributed to the speaker using a reporting verb such as 'said', 'asked', or 'shouted'. Finally, the first letter of the first word of the speech should be capitalized. For example, "I love ice cream," said John.

Rules for Using Indirect Speech

Indirect speech also has some rules that should be followed. First, the tense of the reporting verb should be changed to reflect the time of the original speech. For example, if the original speech was in the past tense, the reporting verb should also be in the past tense. Second, the word 'that' is used to introduce the speaker's words. For example, John said that he loves ice cream. Third, the pronouns should be changed to reflect the speaker's words. For example, "I love ice cream," said John would become John said that he loves ice cream. Finally, no quotation marks are used in indirect speech.

Consider the following examples

- Peter said that he wanted to eat ice cream.
- Ria said that she worked as a doctor on the army campus.
- Our teacher asked us if we wanted to go to the games.
- The principal asked us to leave the ground immediately

Conversion from direct to indirect speech

What is Direct & Indirect Speech?

Direct speech – reporting the message of the speaker in the exact words as spoken by him.
Direct speech example: Maya said, 'I am busy now'.
Indirect speech: reporting the message of the speaker in our own words.
Indirect speech example: Maya said that she was busy then.

Direct And Indirect Speech Rules

Rules for converting Direct into Indirect speech.

To change a sentence of direct speech into indirect speech there are various factors that are considered, such as reporting verbs, modals, time, place, pronouns, tenses, etc. We will discuss each of these factors one by one.

Rule 1 – Direct to Indirect Speech Conversion – Reporting Verb

1. When the reporting verb of direct speech is in past tense then all the present tenses are changed to the corresponding past tense in indirect speech.

Direct to indirect speech example:

Direct: She said, 'I am happy'.

1. Indirect: She said (that) she was happy.

In indirect speech, tenses do not change if the words used within the quotes ('') talk of a habitual action or universal truth.

Direct to indirect speech example:

Direct: He said, 'We cannot live without air'.

Indirect: He said that we cannot live without air.

1. The tenses of direct speech do not change if the reporting verb is in the future tense or present tense.

Direct to indirect speech example:

Direct: She says/will say, 'I am going'

Indirect: She says/will say she is going.

Rule 2 – Direct Speech to Indirect Speech conversion – Present Tense

- **Present Perfect Changes to Past Perfect.**

Direct to indirect speech example:

Direct: "I have been to Boston", she told me.

Indirect: She told me that she had been to Boston.

- **Present Continuous Changes to Past Continuous**

Direct to indirect speech example:

Direct: "I am playing the guitar", she explained.

Indirect: She explained that she was playing the guitar.

- **Present Perfect Changes to Past Perfect**

Direct to indirect speech example:

Direct: He said, "She has finished her homework ".

Indirect: He said that she had finished her homework.

- **Simple Present Changes to Simple Past**

Direct to indirect speech example:

Direct: "I am unwell", she said.

Indirect: She said that she was unwell.

Rule 3 – Direct Speech to Indirect Speech conversion – Past Tense & Future Tense

- **Simple Past Changes to Past Perfect**

Direct to indirect speech example:

Direct: She said, "Irvin arrived on Sunday."

Indirect: She said that Irvin had arrived on Sunday.

- **Past Continuous Changes to Past Perfect Continuous**

Direct to indirect speech example

Direct: "We were playing basketball", they told me.

Indirect: They told me that they had been playing basketball.

- **Future Changes to Present Conditional**

Direct to indirect speech example

Direct: She said, “I will be in Scotland tomorrow.”
Indirect: She said that she would be in Scotland the next day.

- **Future Continuous Changes to Conditional Continuous**

Direct to indirect speech example
Direct: He said, “I’ll be disposing of the old computer next Tuesday.”
Indirect: He said that he would be disposing of the old computer the following Tuesday.

Rule 4 – Direct Speech to Indirect Speech Conversion – Interrogative Sentences

- No conjunction is used, if a sentence in direct speech begins with a question (what/where/when) as the “question-word” itself acts as a joining clause.

Direct to indirect speech example
Direct: “Where do you live?” asked the boy.
Indirect: The boy enquired where I lived.
If a direct speech sentence begins with an auxiliary verb/helping verb, the joining clause should be if or whether.

Direct to indirect speech example
Direct: She said, ‘Will you come for the party’?
Indirect: She asked whether we would come for the party.

- Reporting verbs such as ‘said/ said to’ changes to enquired, asked, or demanded.

Direct to indirect speech example
Direct: He said to me, ‘What are you wearing’?
Indirect: He asked me what I was wearing.

Rule 5 – Direct Speech to Indirect Speech Conversion – Changes in Modals
While changing direct speech to indirect speech, the modals used in the sentences change like:

1. Can becomes could.
2. May becomes might.
3. Must becomes had to /would have to.

Check the examples:

- Direct: She said, ‘She **can** dance’.

- Indirect: She said that she **could** dance.
- Direct: She said, 'I **may** buy a dress'.
- Indirect: She said that she **might** buy a dress.
- Direct: Rama said, 'I **must** complete the assignment'.
- Indirect: Rama said that he **had to** complete the assignment.

There are modals that **do not change** – Could, Would, Should, Might, Ought to

- Direct: She said, 'I should clean the house'
- Indirect: She said that she should clean the house.

Rule 6 – Direct Speech to Indirect Speech Conversion – Pronoun

1. The first person in direct speech changes as per the subject of the speech.

Direct speech to indirect speech examples-

Direct: He said, "I am in class Twelfth."

Indirect: He says that he was in class Twelfth.

1. The second person of direct speech changes as per the object of reporting speech.

Direct speech to indirect speech examples –

Direct: She says to them, "You have done your work."

Indirect: She tells them that they have done their work.

1. The third person of direct speech doesn't change.

Direct speech to indirect speech examples –

Direct: He says, "She dances well."

Indirect: He says that she dances well.

Rule 7 – Direct Speech to Indirect Speech Conversion – Request, Command, Wish, Exclamation

1. Indirect Speech is supported by some verbs like requested, ordered, suggested, and advised. Forbid-forbade is used for negative sentences. Therefore, the imperative mood in the direct speech changes into the Infinitive in indirect speech.

Direct: She said to her 'Please complete it'.

Indirect: She requested her to complete it.

Direct: Hamid said to Ramid, 'Sit down'.

Indirect: Hamid ordered Ramid to sit down.

1. In **Exclamatory sentences** that express grief, sorrow, happiness, applaud, **Interject ions are removed,** and the sentence is **changed to an assertive sentence.**

Direct: She said, 'Alas! I am undone'.

Indirect: She exclaimed sadly that she was broke.

Rule 8 – Direct Speech to Indirect Speech Conversion – Punctuations

1. In direct speech, the words actually spoken should be in ('') quotes and always begin with a capital letter.

Example: She said, "I am the best."

1. Full stop, comma, exclamation, or question mark are placed inside the closing inverted commas.

Example: They asked, "Can we sing with you?"

1. If direct speech comes after the information about who is speaking, a comma is used to introduce the speech, placed before the first inverted comma.

Direct speech example: He shouted, "Shut up!

Direct speech example: "Thinking back," he said, "she didn't expect to win." (Comma is used to separate the two direct speeches and no capital letter to begin the second sentence).

Rule 9 – Direct Speech to Indirect Speech Conversion – Change of Time

1. In direct speeches, the words that express nearness in time or place are changed to words that express distance in indirect speech. Such as:

- Now becomes then
- Here becomes there
- Ago becomes before
- Thus, becomes so
- Today becomes that day
- Tomorrow becomes the next day
- This becomes that
- Yesterday becomes the day before
- These become those
- Hither becomes thither
- Come becomes go
- Hence becomes thence
- Next week or month becomes following week/month

Examples:

Direct: He said, 'His girlfriend came yesterday.'

Indirect: He said that his girlfriend had come the day before.

1. The time expression does not change if the reporting verb is in the present tense or future tense.

Examples:

Direct: He says/will say, 'My girlfriend came yesterday.'

Indirect: He says/will say that his girlfriend had come the day before.

Rules of converting Indirect Speech into Direct Speech

1. The following rules should be followed while converting an indirect speech to direct speech:
2. Use the reporting verb such as (say, said to) in its correct tense.
3. Put a comma before the statement and the first letter of the statement should be in capital letter.
4. Insert question mark, quotation marks, exclamation mark and full stop, based on the mood of the sentence.
5. Remove the conjunctions like (that, to, if or whether) wherever necessary.
6. Where the reporting verb is in past tense in indirect, change it to present tense in the direct speech.
7. Change the past perfect tense either into present perfect tense or past tense, as necessary.

Check the examples:

- Indirect: She asked whether she was coming to the prom night.
- Direct: She said to her, "Are you coming to the prom night?"
- Indirect: The girl said that she was happy with her result.
- Direct: The girl said. "I am happy with my result."

Punctuation in Direct Speech

In direct speech, punctuation is essential to accurately convey the speaker's message. Commas, full stops, exclamation marks, and question marks should be placed inside the quotation marks, depending on the context. For example, "I can't believe it!" exclaimed John. In this example, the exclamation mark is placed inside the quotation marks because it belongs to the direct speech.

Changing Tenses in Indirect Speech

One of the most important rules of indirect speech is to change the tense of the reporting verb to match the time of the original speech. When converting direct speech to indirect speech, tense changes are often required to reflect the change in time from when the speaker originally said it to when it is being reported. Here is some common tense changes.

- Present tense changes to past tense.
- Past tense changes to past perfect tense.
- Present continuous tense changes to past continuous tense.
- Future tense changes to conditional tense.

Reporting Verbs

Reporting verbs are essential in narration because they help to identify the speaker and the message they are conveying. The most common reporting verbs used in direct and indirect speech include 'said', 'asked', 'shouted', 'whispered', 'told', 'suggested', 'advised', 'warned', 'promised', and 'agreed'. It is important to choose the appropriate reporting verb to accurately convey the speaker's message and tone.

Reporting Statements, Questions, and Commands

Direct and indirect speech can be used to report statements, questions, and commands. When reporting statements, the speaker's words are retold in the same order as they were spoken. When reporting questions, the word order is changed to form a statement, and the reporting verb is followed by 'if' or 'whether'. When reporting commands, the verb in the reporting clause is changed to 'tell' or 'order'. Here are some examples

Reporting Statements:
Direct Speech: "I have a meeting at 3 pm," said John.
Indirect Speech: John said that he had a meeting at 3 pm.

Reporting Questions:
Direct Speech: "Are you going to the party?" asked Jane.
Indirect Speech: Jane asked if I was going to the party.

Reporting Commands:

Direct Speech: "Please come to my office," said the boss.

Indirect Speech: The boss told me to come to his office.

MULTIPLE CHOICE QUESTION

Direction (1 - 5): Each item in this section has a direct statement followed by its reported form in indirect speech. Select the correct statement in indirect speech and mark it in the Answer Sheet accordingly.

1. The captain said to his soldiers, "Move forward and face the target now."

A. The captain ordered his soldiers to move forward and face the target.

B. The captain asked his soldiers to move forward and face the target then.

C. The captain told his soldiers that they move forward and face the target immediately.

D. The captain informed his soldiers that they should move forward and face the target now.

Answer: C

Explanation:

The original sentence is direct speech, this needs to be converted to indirect speech. The original sentence mentions a captain and soldiers implying that the statement will be an order. Thus option 2 cannot be the answer as it is information, not an order. Option 3 cannot be the answer as the verb 'asked' implies a question, not an order. Option 4 cannot be the answer is missing the adverb 'now', thus not informing us about the timing of the action.

2. Vivek said to his friend, "Could you please turn off the switch ?"

A. Vivek told his friend to turn off the switch

B. Vivek requested his friend to turn off the switch

C. Vivek told his friend that he should turn off the switch

D. Vivek asked his friend to please turn off the switch

Answer: B

Explanation:

The statement in the direct speech is a request made in the interrogative form, so the use of the verb 'requested' will be suitable in indirect speech.

3. The preacher said to the crowd, "The Sun rises every day for all of us without any expectations in return."

A. The preacher told the crowd that the Sun rose every day for all of them without any expectations in return.

B. The preacher told the crowd that the Sun has risen every day for all of them without any expectations in return.

C. The preacher told the crowd that the Sun rises every day for all of them without any expectations in return

D. The preacher told the crowd that the Sun rises every day for all of us without any expectations in return

Answer: C

Explanation:

As the information in the direct speech statement is a universal fact thus it remains in simple present tense even after conversion to indirect speech.

This only leaves options C and D possible.

Option D is eliminated as it uses the phrase 'all of us.'

4. Romila said to Rahim, "Where were your ideas when we faced the troubles last week ?"

A. Romila asked Rahim where his ideas had been when they had faced the trouble the week before

B. Romila requested Rahim where his ideas had been when they faced the trouble the week before

C. Romila told Rahim where his ideas were when they faced the trouble the week before

D. Romila asked Rahim where his ideas had been when they faced the trouble the last week

Answer: A

Explanation:

The statement in direct speech is a question which Romila is asking to Rahim.

So, only options A and D are suitable. The past indefinite tense in direct speech gets converted to past perfect tense in indirect speech.

Out of the available options, only option A satisfies both these criteria and thus is the correct response.

5. The actor said to his co-star, Sarita, "Will you go with me for a cup of tea in the evening today?"

A. The actor said to his co-star if she would go for a cup of tea with him in evening today

B. The actor requests his co-star, Sarita if she would go with him for a cup of tea in that evening that day

C. The actor asked his co-star Sarita if she would go with him for a cup of tea in the evening that day

D. The actor told his co-star, Sarita if she would go with him for a cup of tea in evening that day

Answer: C

Explanation:

The direct speech statement is in the form of a question, so the verb 'ask' in past participle form is the most viable option.

Directions (6-20):

In each of the following questions, a sentence has been given in direct/indirect speech. Out of the four alternatives suggested select the one which best expresses the same sentence in indirect/ direct speech.

6. He said to her, "Don't read so fast."

A. He requested her not to read so fast.

B. He advised her don't read so fast.

C. He ordered her not to read so fast.

D. He told her not to read so fast.

Answer: D

Explanation:

The word 'requested' can be used in indirect speech if 'begged' or 'please' is used in direct speech. 'Ordered' may be used in indirect speech if an exclamation mark or the word 'ordered' is used in direct speech.

7. She said that it had happened ten days before.

A. She said, "It has happened ten days before."

B. She said, "It happened ten days ago."

C. She said, "It happens ten days ago."

D. She said, "It happened ten days before."

Answer: B

Explanation:

The given sentence is indirect speech. The correct Narration is “She said, "It happened ten days ago."

8. "Why are you looking through the keyhole?" I said.
A. I said to him that why he was looking through the keyhole.
B. I said to him why he is looking through the keyhole.
C. I asked you why you are looking through the keyhole.
D. I asked him why he was looking through the keyhole.

Answer: D
Explanation:
The given sentence is in direct speech. The correct Narration is "I asked him why he was looking through the keyhole."

9. He said to me, "Where is the post office?"
A. He asked me where the post office was.
B. He asked me that where the post office was.
C. He asked me where the post office was.
D. He wanted to know where the post office was.

Answer: A
Explanation:
The given sentence is in direct speech. The correct Narration is "He asked me where the post office was."

10. He said that those oranges were stale.
A. He said, "These oranges are stale."
B. He said, "Those oranges are stale."
C. He mentioned, "These oranges are stale."
D. He told, "The oranges are stale."

Answer: A
Explanation:
'Those' in indirect speech. The correct narration is He said, "These oranges are stale."

11. He said, "What a beautiful scene!"
A. He exclaimed what a beautiful scene it was.

B. He wondered that it was a beautiful scene.
C. He exclaimed that it was a beautiful scene.
D. He said that what a beautiful scene it was.

Answer: C
Explanation:
As the exclamation mark is used in direct speech, the word 'exclaimed' should be used in indirect speech.

12. Rajesh said, "I bought a car yesterday."
A. Rajesh said that he bought a car the previous day.
B. Rajesh told that he had bought a car yesterday.
C. Rajesh said that he had bought a car the previous day.
D. Rajesh said that I have bought a car the previous day.

Answer: C
Explanation:
'Yesterday' would become 'the previous day' in indirect speech. The correct narration is Rajesh said that he had bought a car the previous day.

13. She said she would have the one near her.
A. "I shall have the one near this," she said.
B. "I would have all this," she said.
C. "I'll have this one," she said.
D. "I wanted this one," she said.

Answer: C
Explanation:
The given sentence is in indirect speech. 'The one near him/her' in indirect speech becomes 'this one' in direct speech.

14. He said to her, "Are you coming to the party?"
A. He asked her if she was coming to the party.
B. He told her if she was coming to the party.
C. He asked her if she will be coming to the party.
D. He asked her whether if she was coming to the party.

Ans: A

Explanation:

The correct narration is He asked her if she was coming to the party.

15. He said, "I have often told you not to waste your time."

A. He said that he had often suggested to him not to waste his time.

B. He said that he had often told him not to waste his time.

C. He told that he had often told him not to waste time.

D. He said that he had often told not to waste your time.

Answer: B

Explanation:

The given sentence is in direct speech. The correct narration is He said that he had often told him not to waste his time.

16. "If you don't keep quiet, I shall shoot you," he said to her in a calm voice.

A. He warned her calmly that he would shoot her if she didn't keep quiet.

B. He said calmly that I shall shoot you if you don't be quiet.

C. Calmly he warned her that be quiet or else he will have to shoot her.

D. He warned her to shoot if she didn't keep quiet calmly.

Answer: A

Explanation:

The correct narration is He warned her calmly that he would shoot her if she didn't keep quiet.

17. "What did you eat for breakfast today?" the doctor asked the patient.

A. The doctor asked the patient whether he has eaten breakfast that day.

B. The doctor asked the patient what he had eaten for breakfast that day.

C. The doctor asked the patient whether he was eaten breakfast that day.

D. The doctor asked the patient whether he had eaten breakfast that day.

Answer: B

Explanation:

The correct narration is the doctor asked the patient what he had eaten for breakfast that day.

18. Rohit said, "I need some money."
A. Rohit wanted some money.
B. Rohit said that he would need some money.
C. Rohit was in need of some money.
D. Rohit said that he needed some money.

Answer: D
Explanation:
The given sentence is in direct speech. The correct narration is Rohit said that he needed some money.

19. My cousin said, "My roommate snored throughout the night."
A. My cousin complained to me that her roommate is snoring throughout the night.
B. My cousin told me that her roommate snored throughout the night.
C. My cousin felt that her roommate may be snoring throughout the night.
D. My cousin said that her roommate had snored throughout the night.

Answer: D
Explanation:
The correct narration is My cousin said that her roommate had snored throughout the night.

20. He said to her, "May you succeed!"
A. He wished her success.
B. He prayed to God that she may Succeed.
C. He said to her that she might Succeed.
D. He told her that she might succeed.

Answer: A
Explanation:
The correct narration is He wished her success.

Direction (21-25)

Choose the correct indirect speech for the following direct speech.

21. "I will go to the beach tomorrow," said Emily.

A. Emily said that she will go to the beach tomorrow.

B. Emily said that she would go to the beach tomorrow.

C. Emily says that she would go to the beach tomorrow.

D. Emily says that she will go to the beach tomorrow.

Answer: B

Explanation:

In indirect speech, the correct narration is Emily said that she would go to the beach tomorrow.

22. "I am going to the market now," said Sarah.

A. Sarah said that she will go to the market now.

B. Sarah said that she would go to the market then.

C. Sarah said that she is going to the market now.

D. Sarah said that she was going to the market then.

Answer: D

Explanation:

The correct narration is Sarah said that she was going to the market then.

23. "I have never been to Paris," said Jane.

A. Jane said that she had never been to Paris.

B. Jane says that she had never been to Paris.

C. Jane said that she has never been to Paris.

D. Jane says that she has never been to Paris.

Answer: A

Explanation:

The correct narration is Jane said that she had never been to Paris.

24. "I am studying for my exam," said Tom.

A. Tom said that he is studying for his exam.

B. Tom said that he was studying for his exam.

C. Tom said, "I am studying for my exam."
D. Tom said to me that he is studying for his exam.

Answer: B
Explanation:
In indirect speech, the correct narration is Tom said that he was studying for his exam.

25. "I will not attend the meeting tomorrow," said the manager.
A. The manager said that he will not attend the meeting tomorrow.
B. The manager said that he would not attend the meeting the next day.
C. The manager said, "I will not attend the meeting tomorrow."
D. The manager said to his assistant that he will not attend the meeting tomorrow.

Answer: B
Explanation:
In indirect speech, the correct narration is The manager said that he would not attend the meeting the next day.

Direction (26-30)
Choose the correct direct speech for the following indirect speech:
26. The teacher said that the exam would be difficult.
A. "The exam is going to be difficult," said the teacher.
B. "The exam will be difficult," said the teacher.
C. "The exam was going to be difficult," said the teacher.
D. "The exam would be difficult," said the teacher.

Answer: D
Explanation:
In direct speech, the correct narration is "The exam would be difficult," said the teacher.

27. The doctor told me to take rest.
A. "Take rest," said the doctor.
B. "You should take rest," said the doctor.
C. "You must take rest," said the doctor.
D. "I am telling you to take a rest," said the doctor.

Answer: A
Explanation:
The correct narration is "Take rest," said the doctor.

28. The teacher told the students not to talk during the exam.
A. "Do not talk during the exam," said the teacher to the students.
B. "You should not talk during the exam," said the teacher to the students.
C. "You must not talk during the exam," said the teacher to the students.
D. "I am telling you not to talk during the exam," said the teacher to the students.

Answer: A
Explanation:
The correct narration is "Do not talk during the exam," said the teacher to the students.

29. The waiter told us to order quickly.
A. "Order quickly," said the waiter.
B. "You should order quickly," said the waiter.
C. "You must order quickly," said the waiter.
D. "I am telling you to order quickly," said the waiter.

Answer: A
Explanation:
The correct narration is "Order quickly," said the waiter.

30. She told me that she had never been to Paris before.
A. "I have never been to Paris before," she said to me.
B. "I had never been to Paris before," she said to me.
C. "I have never been to Paris before," I said to her.
D. "I had never been to Paris before," I said to her.

Answer: A
Explanation:
The correct narration is "I have never been to Paris before," she said to me.

SENTENCE IMPROVEMENT

Definition of Sentence Improvement

- Sentence improvement refers to the process of revising and refining a sentence to make it more effective, clear, and engaging for the reader.
- This process involves identifying areas where the sentence can be improved, such as by correcting grammatical errors, refining the choice of vocabulary, simplifying complex ideas, or adjusting the tone and style to match the intended audience.
- Sentence improvement can be an iterative process, involving multiple rounds of revision and refinement to achieve the desired level of clarity and effectiveness.
- It is an essential component of effective writing, as it enables the writer to communicate their message in a way that is clear, concise, and engaging to the reader.
- Some common techniques used in sentence improvement include restructuring sentences to emphasize key ideas, using active voice instead of passive voice, varying the sentence length and structure to create rhythm and flow, and eliminating unnecessary words and phrases.
- Ultimately, the goal of sentence improvement is to create writing that is clear, effective, and engaging, and that effectively conveys the writer's intended message to the reader.

Examples: For Sentence Improvement

Example: 1. He felt exhausted as **he was working** since 4 O' clock in the morning

A. Has been working.

B. Had been working.

C. Is working.

D. No improvement.

Answer: B (As the past perfect continuous tense will be used.)

Example: 2. Most people in India like to give a lot of free **advice**.
A. Advice
B. Advises
C. Advise
D. No improvement

Answer: D (The word advice is a noun and has no plural form. Advise is a verb. So, option a, b and C all get eliminated)

Example: 3. Hardly had he finished his work **than** the peon arrived with another file.
A. When
B. Then
C. While
D. No improvement

Answer: A (With hardly the word when is used)

Example: 4. Rahul has no right **to take a claim** on his father's property as he did not look after him in his old age.
A. To make a claim
B. To stake a claim to
C. To demand
D. No improvement

Answer: B (stake a claim is a phrase which means to ask for something as one's own)

Example: 5. I **have sent** the parcel two hours ago.
A. Had sent
B. Send
C. Sent
D. No improvement

Answer: C (The usage of two hours ago indicates that the sentence if of simple past tense)

Sentence Improvement Terms

- **Grammar:** Refers to the rules and principles governing the structure of words and their arrangement in sentences.
- **Syntax:** Refers to the way words are arranged to form sentences.
- **Punctuation:** Refers to the use of marks such as periods, commas, and colons to clarify the meaning of sentences and improve readability.
- **Clarity:** Refers to the degree to which a sentence can be easily understood by the reader.
- **Conciseness:** Refers to the use of few words to convey a message.
- **Coherence:** Refers to the logical connections between sentences or ideas in a text.
- **Tone:** Refers to the writer's attitude towards the subject matter, which is conveyed through the language used.
- **Voice:** Refers to the relationship between the subject of the sentence and the action being performed, which can be either active or passive.
- **Diction:** Refers to the choice and use of words in writing, including vocabulary and phrasing.

Rules of Sentence Improvement

There are no fixed rules for sentence improvement as the strategies used will depend on the specific context and purpose of the writing. However, here are some general guidelines that can help writers improve their sentences:

1. **Subject-Verb Agreement**

   Under this, if the subject in the sentence is in the singular form, then the verb will also be in the singular form and if the subject is in the plural form, then the verb will also be in a plural form.

   Example

   - The boy is playing in the playing ground – here, "boy" is singular, hence it takes a singular verb "is".
   - The parents know how to handle their naughty kids – here, "parents" is plural hence takes a plural verb "know"
   - Anybody is more fun than you – here, "anybody" is singular hence it takes a singular verb "is".

- The rats gnaw at the cheese – here, "rats" is plural hence it will take a plural verb "gnaw."
- Both Mita and Rita love to have chocolates – here, with the use of 'and' we see that the two singular subjects 'Mita and 'Rita; become plural hence it will take a plural verb "love."
- Rohan with his guitar and drums plays good music – here, though we use 'and' between two objects -guitar and drums, the subject here is Rohan, which is singular, hence it will take a singular verb "play".

2. **Modifier Words or Clauses**

   Modifier: A modifier is a word that modifies the meaning of a sentence (gives more information) about a particular subject.

   There is main two types of modifiers:

   Adjectives – it modifies a noun.

   Adverb – it modifies verbs, adjectives, or other adverbs.

   Example

   - She is very excited for her new day at work – here, the verb excited is modified by 'very' which shows the extent of her excitement.
   - The room was beautifully decorated for the festival – here the verb decorated is modified with 'beautifully'.
   - Sarah was a sure fit for the dance group – here the verb fit is modified by the word 'sure'.
   - She practiced her session in the auditorium – here the noun sessions are modified by the collective adverb 'in the auditorium' thus modifying the place of session.

3. **Misplaced Modifiers**

   Sometimes modifiers can be used in wrong places that change the subject which has to be modified.

   - Her father bought a pet dog for his daughter named Junnie. – here, it implies that the daughter's name was Junnie.
   - Here father bout a pet dog named Junnie for his daughter. – Here, it implies that the pet's name was Junnie.

The second sentence is the correct one.

4. **Parallel Elements**

   It says that some ideas should be presented in the same grammatical form.

   This means that if a sentence consists of more than one verb then the form of all the verbs should be in the same form. If the starting verb is in simple form, all the verbs should follow the same pattern.

   Example

   - Neha loves to cook, dance and sing – here all the three verbs are in simple present form.
   - Neha loves cooking, dancing, and singing – In this sentence, all the three verbs follow the continuous form of verb.
   - Some men love to sit and relax during travels while some like to work. – here all three four verbs are in the simple present form.
   - Mary went down the stairs and cooked for the men. – here the two verbs are in simple past form.
   - Neither the weather in Mumbai nor the weather in Delhi are improving – here, we use the same form of sentence which is 'the weather in'.
   - The lesson was enriching both to listen and to learn – to listen and to learn is the same form of verb.

5. **Redundancy**

   As per the rules of redundancy, any idea should not be repeated again and again. Repeated words should be avoided to make sentences clear.

   Some of the common Redundant words are given in the lift-

   Foreign imports

   Bald – headed

   Drop – down.

   End – result

   Few in number

   Follow – after

   General – public

   Hurry – up

   Chase – after

But – yet
Collaborate – together

Example

- Three files of monthly statistics were combined into one. – here the word into one is redundant because 'combined' already means to put together'.
- The teacher repeated again the lecture – here again is redundant because repeat already means 'to say it again'
- The thief followed after her – here after is redundant because follow means 'to be behind someone' hence after is unnecessary here.

6. **Pronoun Reference Error**

A pronoun comes after the noun and should be able to refer clearly to one, clear, unmistakable noun. This type of noun is termed as antecedent.

Example

- Jane put the shoes in the rack, but it slid down.
- Here, 'it' can be referred to the 'shoes or the 'wardrobe' hence it's a faulty pronoun. Instead, it should be either,
- 'Jane put the shoes in the rack and the shoes slid down' /or
- 'Jane put the shoes in the rack and the rack slid down.'

Hence, knowing how and where to use the noun-pronoun relation is very important. The three most important errors are:

- **Too Many antecedents**

  Bring the box out of the cabinet and fix it. (Here, it can be referred to either the box or the cabinet, hence too many antecedents can confuse the reader'

- **Hidden Antecedents**

  The soda bottles were empty, but we were tired of drinking it anyway. (Here, it can refer to either soda or bottles, the hidden antecedent 'it' can be said as 'The soda bottles were empty but we were tired of drinking the soda anyway')

- **No antecedent at all**

  The clients called the office several times, but they didn't answer. (Here, they can't be the office, it has to be the receptionists or the employees, hence, they are the hidden antecedents. So, the sentence could be 'The clients called the office several times but the employees didn't answer.'

7. **Wording**

   Wrong use of words may make the whole sentence wrong. Hence selection of the right word at the right place is very important.

   For better understanding, a few diction examples are given below. Try to practice these and other diction words available on the internet to clear all the doubts related to this topic.

   While using wording function it is important to understand the difference between:

   - **Homonyms –** Two or more words having the same spelling or pronunciation but different meaning.
   - **Homophones –** Two or more words having different spelling and meaning but are pronounced alike.

8. **Wrong comparisons**

   Sometimes, the comparisons are made between dissimilar things or in an incorrect way.

   Example

   - John is wiser than all men. (Incorrect way)
   - John is wiser than all other men. (Correct way- John needs to be excluded from the rest of the same category.)
   - In the above example, comparative degree is used. But in case of superlative degree, the person/thing compared is included in the rest of the class. E.g., John is the strongest of all men.
   - Overall, you need to make sure that the different parts of speech (adjectives, adverbs, nouns, pronouns, conjunctions, interjections, verbs, etc.) are used appropriately and at the right place in the sentence.
   - So now, you are aware of the errors that may occur in questions based on sentence correction. The next step should be to devise a strategy to answer these questions in an accurate and timely manner. Keep the following things in mind while tackling a sentence correction question:

Identify the concept

- The very reason above-stated rules were discussed! Generally, in such questions, one or two rules are rules are used inappropriately. So, the first task is to identify the particular kind of error/s.
- Keep an eye on the time indicators (before, after, during, etc.). This can help you spot the verb tense errors easily. In some cases, the whole sentence needs to be rewritten.
- Once you have figured out the kind of error/s, try to make the correction without looking at the options.

9. **Use correct grammar**
   Make sure to follow the rules of grammar, such as using proper subject-verb agreement, avoiding sentence fragments, and using appropriate verb tenses.

10. **Be concise**
    Use as few words as possible to convey the message. Avoid using unnecessary words or phrases that don't add value to the sentence.

11. **Use active voice**
    In general, active voice is more engaging and easier to understand than passive voice. Use active voice whenever possible to make the sentence more direct and engaging.

12. **Vary sentence length and structure**
    Use a mix of short and long sentences, as well as different sentence structures, to create rhythm and flow in the writing.

13. **Eliminate jargon and technical language**
    Avoid using complex or technical language that the reader may not understand. Use simple and clear language that is easy to understand.

14. **Use transitional words and phrases**
    Use transitional words and phrases such as however", "therefore", and "in addition" to help the reader understand the relationship between different ideas in the text.

15. **Proofread and edit**
    After writing, carefully proofread and edit the text to ensure that it free of errors and flows smoothly.

Fundamentals Of Sentence Improvement

The fundamentals of sentence improvement involve identifying areas of the sentence that can be revised or refined to make it more effective, clear, and engaging for the reader. Here are some of the kcy fundamentals of sentence improvement:

1. **Understand the purpose and audience**
   Before starting to write, it's important to have a clear understanding of the purpose of the text and the intended audience. This will help guide the choice of vocabulary, tone, and style.

2. **Focus on clarity**
   A clear sentence is one that can be easily understood by the reader. To improve clarity, make sure to use simple and concise language, avoid jargon, and use active voice whenever possible.

3. **Pay attention to sentence structure**
   The structure of a sentence can have a big impact on its effectiveness. Vary sentence length and structure to create rhythm and flow, and use transitional words and phrases to connect different ideas.

4. **Eliminate errors**
   Grammatical errors and spelling mistakes can distract the reader and undermine the credibility of the writer. Carefully proofread the text to ensure that it is free of errors.

5. **Refine vocabulary and style**
   The choice of words and the overall style of writing can have a big impact on how engaging and effective the text is. Use appropriate vocabulary for the audience, and refine the style to create a more engaging and persuasive message.

6. **Consider the tone and voice**
   The tone and voice of the sentence should match the intended audience, purpose, and context of the communication. Use language that is appropriate for the tone and voice of the message.

Difference Between Sentence Improvement or Sentence Correction

- Sentence improvement and sentence correction are both important aspects of writing, but they have different goals and approaches.
- Sentence improvement focuses on refining and enhancing a sentence to make it more effective, clear, and engaging for the reader. This might involve improving the sentence structure, refining the vocabulary, varying the sentence length, and so on.
- The goal of sentence improvement is to create writing that is clear, concise, and persuasive.
- Sentence correction, on the other hand, focuses on identifying and fixing errors in a sentence. This might involve correcting grammar, spelling, punctuation, or syntax mistakes.
- The goal of sentence correction is to ensure that the sentence is free of errors and can be easily understood by the reader.
- While both sentence improvement and sentence correction are important, they have different goals and approaches.
- Sentence improvement is about refining and enhancing the sentence to make it more effective and persuasive, while sentence correction is about identifying and fixing errors to ensure that the sentence is clear and easily understood.
- Sentence improvement is an important aspect of grammar because it helps to refine and enhance the effectiveness of the sentence.
- Good writing requires not only correct grammar and punctuation but also effective sentence structure, clarity, and coherence.

Here are some reasons why sentence improvement is important in grammar

- **Enhances clarity:** A well-crafted sentence is one that can be easily understood by the reader. By improving sentence structure, vocabulary, and length, writers can create sentences that are clear, concise, and effective in communicating their message.
- **Creates engagement:** A well-written sentence can capture the reader's attention and create engagement. By varying sentence structure and using appropriate vocabulary and style, writers can create a more engaging message that draws the reader in.
- **Improves coherence:** A well-structured sentence can help to create coherence and flow in the writing. By using transitional words and phrases and varying sentence length and structure, writers can create a more cohesive message that is easy to follow.

- **Demonstrates professionalism:** good writing skills, including effective sentence improvement, are highly valued in many professions. By demonstrating strong writing skills, writers can enhance their professional image and credibility.
- **Supports effective communication:** Effective sentence improvement is essential for effective communication. By creating clear, engaging, and coherent messages, writers can convey their intended meaning to the reader and achieve their communication goals.

Many people have doubts related to sentence improvement. It is not always easy to remember the grammatical and punctuational rules.

Incorrect Sentence Formation

Before we tell you how you can incorporate sentence improvement in your writing it's important to understand what exactly incorrect sentence formation is.

Mainly there are two types of mistakes that you will make while writing a sentence:

1. **Run-on sentences:** When you use incorrect punctuation to join two sentences.
2. **Sentence fragments:** When your sentence is missing necessary words to make complete sense.

It's extremely important to write grammatically correct sentences that have a clear message. If we write grammatically incorrect sentences, then the meaning of the sentence completely changes.

Many people are not able to express their ideas clearly in the form of words. The root problem is sentence formation.

Most people think that sentence formation is only restricted to grammar. This is not at all true! Your style and flow of writing along with the words you choose to write matters a lot. To be very Frank, if you have common sense and a bit of knowledge of grammar you can ace sentence formation.

How to Avoid Run-on Sentence Error?

Independent clauses are a group of words that don't need any other sentence to make full sense. These sentences can stand alone and still be clear in their messaging.

Run-on sentence error occurs when you join two independent clauses with incorrect punctuation.

Adding Unnecessary Comma

You cannot join two independent clauses with a comma without placing conjunction. This type of error is known as a comma splice. You can fix this error in four ways

1. **Replace the comma with a semicolon**
   - This is one of the easiest ways to fix the comma splice error. Simply replace the comma with a semicolon and link the two sentences.

2. **Add conjunction**
   - Conjunctions are the traditional way to join two Sentences. You can use both the coordinating and subordinating conjunctions.
   - Some common examples of conjunctions are but, because, although, or, and, for, when and unless.

3. **Write another sentence**
   - If you think the sentence is expressing two different ideas, then you can replace the comma with a punctuation mark and write two complete sentences.

4. **Let's see these techniques in action**
   - Dancing is my passion; I love learning new dancing moves.
   - You can fix this sentence by using the first technique. Simply, replace the comma with a semicolon.

   Corrected sentence
   - Dancing is my passion; I love learning new dancing moves.
   - Many people like playing games, I like reading books.
   - Just add a coordinating conjunction after the comma.

   Corrected sentence
   - Many people like playing games, but I like reading books.
   - I am staying in the house, it's raining.
   - Both of the sentences are dependent on each other. To fix this we need to add subordinating conjunction.

Corrected sentence

- I am staying in the house because it's raining.
- VPN is not an all-in-one solution; we should always be alert and use different and strong passwords everywhere.
- You can break up this sentence and create two sentences.

Corrected sentence

- VPN is not an all-in-one solution. We should always be alert and use different and strong passwords everywhere.

Missing Comma with a Coordinating Conjunction

Adding coordinating conjunctions without a comma can create run-on errors in your sentences. If you don't add commas, it creates confusion in the minds of readers. The comma helps the reader navigate through your sentences smoothly.

Incorrect sentence: Students should take internships seriously but should also make sure that they give enough time to studies as well.

Correct sentence: Students should take internships seriously but should also make sure that they give enough time to studies as well.

If you use these techniques, then you can learn sentence improvement with ease.

Sentence Fragments

- A sentence fragment is created when your sentence doesn't have all the necessary words to make the sentence grammatically correct. All the sentences must have a subject and a predicate.
- Most of the time the subject always comes before the predicate. You must always remember that every subject needs a predicate, and every predicate needs a subject.

Example

Writing is my passion.

Subject: Writing

Predicate: is my passion

You can create sentence fragments in 2 ways:

1. **The Sentence Doesn't Have Predicate**

   A sentence missing a main verb is the most common form of sentence fragment that blocks your path to sentence improvement. Every Sentence must have a predicate to make complete meaning.

   You can fix this error by adding appropriate punctuation to join the two sentences. The second way is to rewrite the entire sentence by adding a predicate in it.

Incorrect sentence: After doing dance practice for weeks, one of the dancers got injured before the competition. An unpredictable event for everyone.

Correct sentence: After doing dance practice for weeks, one of the dancers got injured before the competition: an unpredictable event for everyone.
(Here, we have added a semicolon to connect the two sentences)

After doing dance practice for weeks, one of the dancers got injured before the competition. It was an unpredictable event for everyone.
(Here, we have rewritten the whole sentence)

2. **Just Writing a Dependent Clause**

   A dependent clause needs an independent clause to form a full sentence. To fix this error you can add subordinating conjunctions: since, while, although, when, after, since, because, while, if, unless, and whereas.

Incorrect sentence: They would start attending colleges. When the cases of coronavirus start decreasing.

Correct sentence: They would start attending colleges when the cases of coronavirus start decreasing.
As you can see, using subordinating clauses correctly can bring sentence improvement in your writing.

Conclusion

To write contextually correct and grammatically sound language, one should know the rules of correct use of language. One must follow the grammatical rules and punctuation efficiently. With hard work and practice, it is possible to write correct sentences.

MULTIPLE CHOICE QUESTIONS

Directions: In the questions, a part of the sentence is given in Underline. Below are given alternatives to the Underline part at (A), (B) and (C) which may improve the sentence. Choose the correct alternative. In case no improvement is needed your answer is (D).

1. The workers are **hell bent at getting** what is due to them.

A. Hell bent on getting

B. Hell bent for getting

C. Hell bent upon getting

D. No improvement

Answer: C

Explanation:

The workers are hell bent upon getting what is due to them.

2. When it was feared that the serfs might go too far and gain their freedom from serfdom, the protestant leaders joined the princess **at crushing them**.

A. Into crushing

B. In crushing

C. Without crushing

D. No improvement

Answer: B

Explanation:

When it was feared that the serfs might go too far and gain their freedom from serfdom, the protestant leaders joined the princess in crushing them.

3. If **the room had been brighter**, I would have been able to read for a while before bedtime.

A. If the room was brighter

B. If the room are brighter

C. Had the room been brighter

D. No improvement

Answer: C

Explanation:
Had the room been brighter I would have been able to read for a while before bedtime.

4. The record for the biggest tiger hunt has not been **met** since 1911 when Lord Hardinge. then Viceroy of India, shot a tiger than measured 11 feet and 6 inches.

A. Improved
B. Broken
C. Bettered
D. No improvement

Answer: B
Explanation:
The record for the biggest tiger hunt has not been broken since 1911 when Lord Hardinga, then viceroy of India, shot a tiger than measured 11 feet and 6 inches.

5. His powerful desire brought about his downfall.

A. His intense desire
B. His desire for power
C. His fatal desire
D. No improvement

Answer: B
Explanation:
His desire for power brought about his downfall.

6. Will you kindly open **the knot**?

A. Untie
B. Break
C. Loose
D. No improvement

Answer: A
Explanation:
Will you kindly untie the knot?

7. He **sent a word** to me that he would be coming late.

A. Sent word
B. Had sent a word
C. Sent words
D. No improvement

Answer: A
Explanation:
He sent word to me that he would be coming late.

8. John **had told me** that he hasn't done it yet.
A. Told
B. Tells
C. Was telling
D. No improvement

Answer: B
Explanation:
John tells me that he hasn't done it yet.

9. If **he had time** he will call you.
A. Would have
B. Would have had
C. Has
D. No improvement

Answer: C
Explanation:
If he has time he will call you.

10. Will you lend me few rupees in this hour of need?
A. Lend me any rupees
B. Borrow me a few rupees
C. Lend me a few rupees
D. No improvement

Answer: C

Explanation:

Will you lend me a few rupees in this hour of need?

11. Thirty-five miles **are a long way** to walk.

A. Is

B. Was

C. Were

D. No improvement

Answer: A

Explanation:

The singular verb "is" will be used in place of "are" because a singular verb is used with 'cardinal adjective + plural noun'.

12. Neither my son nor **my daughter were able** to help me in my work.

A. Was

B. Are

C. Is

D. No Improvement

Answer: A

Explanation:

The singular verb "was" will be used in place of the plural verb "were" because a singular noun "daughter" is used after nor for which a singular verb is required.

13. If my **mother approve** I will go to goa.

A. Approved

B. Approves

C. Approving

D. No improvement

Answer: B

Explanation:

The singular verb – "approves" will be used in place of the plural verb "approve" because the singular subject my mother has been used after if in the given conditional sentence, thus for the singular subject a singular verb is required.

14. The **Army were trying to control** the crowd.
A. The mob
B. The horde
C. The group
D. No improvement

Answer: A
Explanation:
The mob is used in the place of the crowd. Army is not required to control crowd, but when crowd turn violent, then they are termed as 'mob', and in that case, 'army' will be correct.

15. They were surprised by their **peculiar behaviours**.
A. Behave
B. Behaviour
C. Behaves
D. No improvements

Answer: B
Explanation:
Here we have to use the word "behaviour" at the place of behaviours because behaviour is an uncountable noun, and it is not possible to make its plural form.

16. Sri lankan's players were determined to win the Asia cup.
(a). Sri Lankan
(b) The Sri Lankan
(c) The Sri Lankan's
(d) No improvements

Answer: A
Explanation:
Sri Lankan players will be used in the place of Sri Lankan's players because 'sri lankan' itself has a possessive connotation.

17. They **loved theirself** so much that they thought of no one else
A. Them
B. Themself

C. themselves
D. No improvement.

Answer: C
Explanation:
Here we have to use themselves at the place of theirself because themselves is the reflexive pronoun of they.

18. He bought Mango for Ridhi and **myself**.
A. Mine
B. Me
C. I
D. No improvements.

Answer: B
Explanation:
Here "me" should be used at the place of "myself" because the pronoun of objective case is used after a preposition.

19. The woman **who** they thought to be a noblewoman is a rogue.
A. Whose
B. Whom
C. Which
D. No improvement

Answer: B
Explanation:
The relative pronoun 'whom' will be used in place of the relative pronoun 'who' as there is no verb for which the interrogative pronoun 'who' should be used.

20. I will take with me **whosoever** you choose.
A. Whom
B. Who
C. Whomsoever
D. No improvement

Answer: C

Explanation:

The compound relative pronoun 'whomsoever' is used in place of the compound relative pronoun whosoever.

21. If your mother disapproves of the plan you **should** give it up.

A. Would

B. Will

C. Could

D. No improvement.

Answer: D

Explanation:

The sentence has No improvement because should is as a compulsion to obey your parents.

22. Her father thinks that somebody must have dared her **steal** the car.

A. Stole

B. To steal

C. To stole

D. No improvements.

Answer: B

Explanation:

Here we use "to steal" in place of steal. Because "Dare" is used as a main verb, the infinitive with to (to + V1) is used after it.

23. By reading fastly, I **could finish** the book before the book store closed.

A. Can finish

B. Should finish

C. Managed to finish

D. No improvements.

Answer: C

Explanation:

"Managed to finish" is used at the place of "could finish" because the past event has been explained in the given sentence.

The context of the sentence is 'one action' has been done before 'the other action'. The first action is 'reading fastly' and the second action is 'bookstore closed'.

24. The future generation to the **mars** for their winter vacation.

A. Could fly

B. Will fly

C. Will be able to fly

D. No improvement

Answer: C

Explanation:

"Will be able to fly" will be used in place of "can fly" because the given sentence talks about the future and shows possibility. "Can fly" indicated it is now possible, but this is not the context given in the statement, as 'future generation' is mentioned in the statement.

25. The current situation compelled me **writing** the book.

A. To write

B. To wrote

C. Written

D. No improvements

Answer: A

Explanation:

"To write" will be used in place of writing because an "object + infinitive with to" is always used after the word compel.

26. You cannot withdraw all your money **unless you** do not give a prior notice.

A. Unless you not

B. Unless you

C. Unless not

D. No improvements

Answer: B

Explanation:

"Unless you" should be used in place of "unless you do not". The negative word "not" is not used in unless/until starting clause, because they have negative meaning.

27. Hardly had he finished his homework **than** the principal arrived with another file.

A. When

B. Then

C. So

D. No improvement

Answer: B

Explanation:

Here we have to use "when" in place of "than" because with "hardly" the word "when " should be used.

28. Shivam has no right to **take a claim** on his parents property as he did not look after him in his old age.

A. To take claim

B. Stake a claim

C. To manage a claim

D. No improvements.

Answer: B

Explanation:

Here we have to use "stake a claim" in place of "take a claim" because "stake a claim" is used only when you ask for something which one's own.

29. Most people in Pakistan loves to give a lot of free **advice**.

A. Adviced

B. Advocate

C. Advice

D. No improvement

Answer: D

Explanation:

Here the word advice is an uncountable noun, so it has no plural form.

30. The policeman arrested the robber and **send** him to tihad jail.

A. Sent

B. Sending

C. Ended
D. No improvement.

Answer: A
Explanation:
The past participle form 'sent' will be used at the place of 'send' as the context of the statement is of "past tense".

31. Stocks worthy of rupees one lakh were destroyed in the fire which occurred last night.
A. Stocks worth
B. Stocks worth of
C. Stock worthy
D. No improvement

Answer: B
Explanation:
The correct phrase is 'worth of' not 'worthy of'. Hence (a) is the only correct option.

32. He came in quietly **so that** not to wake the child.
A. As for
B. So as
C. As if
D. No improvement

Answer: A
Explanation:
'So that' is used to get a positive result 'so as not' is used to give the meaning of 'not'. Therefore, in order to get desired meaning of the sentence it should be 'so as' in place of 'so that'.

33. Our team lost the football match, **although** the boys put in a very good performance.
A. Put off
B. Put on
C. Put up
D. No improvement
Answer: B

Explanation:

'Put in' has different meanings in different contexts. As for example,

1. To make a formal offer or declaration, e.g., put in a plea of guilty.
2. To fix equipment or furniture into position so that it can be used. eg, we are having a new shower put in.
3. To interrupt another speaker in order to say something eg, Could I put in a word?
4. To officially make a claim, request etc. eg., the company has put in a claim for damages.

Put on = to dress yourself in something. e.g., Hurry up! Put your shirt on. = to give Somebody the telephone so that they can talk to the person at the other end. e.g., Hi, Dad can you put shashi on? = to apply something to your skin, etc.

Put up = to show a particular level of skill, determination

Put off = to cancel/ to make somebody dislike somebody/something; to disturb somebody.

Thus, it is clear that the bold part should be replaced with option (b).

34. Hardly nothing was offered to the victims of the earthquake.

A. Hardly something

B. Hardly anything

C. Hardly little

D. No improvement

Answer: B

Explanation:

The adverb of frequency "hardly" has a negative meaning. Nothing also implies a negative meaning. Two negatives make the sentence positive.

Therefore, the adverbs of frequency having a negative meaning should be followed by anyone, any, anything etc.

35. Anyone with a little interest in sports is bound to familiar with Sachin Tendulkar's name.

A. Binding to be familiar

B. Binding to familiar

C. Bound to be familiar

D. No improvement

Answer: C

Explanation:

On applying the principle of least deviation, the least deviated options are more likely to be a correct option. Here, among the given options, (b) and (d) are least deviated hence either of the two can be a correct option, at the same time, the remaining two options (a) and (c), cannot be the correct options.

Now, let us consider options (b) and (d). Option (d) cannot be a correct option because it has 'to have familiar'. 'Have' means to 'possess something'.

Familiarity is not something in the form of an object that a man can possess. Hence rule out (d). Now, we are left with (b) only, which is absolutely correct.

36. The battle to rage for some time.

A. Is raging

B. Has been raged

C. Had been raging

D. No improvement

Answer: C

Explanation:

"For" and "Since" are used with perfect or perfect continuous tenses.

The correct tense to be used in the given sentence is past perfect continuous tense. The correct form of the verb is "had + been + raging"

37. William Shakespeare is the greatest of **all other** writers.

A. All the

B. Any other

C. The other

D. No improvement

Answer: A

Explanation:

Since the sentence uses the superlative form, 'greatest', it already includes all other writers in the comparison. Therefore, the word 'other' has to be omitted. The correct choice is 'all the'.

38. You would **have succeeded** if you acted upon my advice.

A. Have acted

B. Had acted
C. Would have acted
D. No improvement

Answer: A
Explanation:
The correct combination of conjunction is "had... would have". Here, in the given sentence 'would have' has been used in the beginning of the sentence, therefore it should be 'had' before 'acted' Therefore the correct option is 'had acted'.

39. She has not written to me or to **some of her** other friends since leaving the country.
A. None of her
B. One of her
C. Any of her
D. No improvement

Answer: B
Explanation:
'Some of her' conveys the meaning of some friends out of many. But the writer wants to convey that "she has written to no one".
Therefore, the correct substitute for 'some of her' is 'any of her'.

40. They were then asked to write a short account of what they **have seen**.
A. Had seen
B. Were seen
C. Had been seen
D. No improvement

Answer: C
Explanation:
The given sentence is in Past Tense. Hence it should be 'had seen' in place of 'have seen'.

41. The surface of the road has got **severe damage** during the heavy rains last week.
A. Has severe damage
B. Getting severely damaged
C. Is been damaged severely

D. Was severely damaged

Answer: D

Explanation:

The 'Last week' suggests the event of past tense. Therefore, ‘getting is’ and ‘getting has ’ used in options (a), (b) and (c) respectively make them grammatically incorrect, hence they are ruled out. Thus, only option (d) is correct.

42. Being injured, one of the migratory birds **have not flown** south.

A. Have not flown

B. Have not flew

C. Does not flew

D. Has not flown

Answer: D

Explanation:

'One of the migratory birds' means ‘one bird out of many birds’.

Hence, for one bird singular verb must be used. The singular of ‘have’ is 'has'. Hence (d) is the correct choice.

43. She and Dad would has **had loved** Amit.

A. Has loved

B. Have loved

C. To loved

D. No improvement

Answer: B

Explanation:

When the subject is plural (she + had) the verb must also be used in plural form.

Therefore, “has had loved” is replaced by “have loved”

44. This milk has got a funny taste — it can **have gone sour**.

A. May have gone sour

B. Can go sour

C. Had soured

D. No improvement

Answer: C

Explanation:

'Can' gives a sense of more certainty than 'may'. The milk may or may not have gone sour. There is a doubt. We cannot say with certainty that milk has gone sour. So it is better to use 'may have gone sour' than 'can have gone sour'.

45. It has **being** too dangerous for too many people.

A. To be

B. Become

C. Be

D. No improvement

Answer: B

Explanation:

"Has" should be followed by the past participle form of the verb which is "become" here.

46. The season being very favourable, he seems to **have been enjoyed** the vacation.

A. Be enjoyed

B. Have enjoyed

C. Have been enjoy

D. Had been enjoyed

Answer: B

Explanation:

After 'have/has/had' V3 is used. Hence, the phrase in bold should be replaced with 'have enjoyed'. Thus, (a) is correct.

47. Sudha was determined to get a better job, in **pursuing higher** studies.

A. Pursuing higher

B. By pursuing higher

C. In the pursuit of high

D. To pursuit higher

Answer: A

Explanation:

'Pursue' (verb) cannot be replaced by 'pursuit' (noun). Hence options (b) and (d) are ruled out.

The phrase in bold may be replaced by option (c) because option (d) has 'by' which is superfluous.

48. With rising prices people find it difficult to make **both the ends** meet.
A. Both ends
B. The both ends
C. Both their ends
D. No improvement

Answer: B
Explanation:
The correct phrase is 'to make both ends meet'. Therefore, the use of 'the' is superfluous. Hence replace bold part with 'both ends', i.e., option (B).

49. They could not admire his bright performance because **they dislike him**.
A. Because of their disliking of
B. Because of their dislike
C. Because they dislike
D. As they have disliked

Answer: C
Explanation:

The given sentence is the combination of two simple sentences:
(i) They dislike him.
(ii) They could not admire his bright performance.
To join the above two sentences 'because' has been used. The phrase in bold can be replaced by option (C) because this option is most similar to the phrase in bold. Other options are widely deviated and cannot be the correct choice.

50. She was uneasy because she **had never been** on a plane before.
A. Had never been
B. Never been
C. Is never been
D. No improvement

Answer: A
Explanation:
When two actions are in the past tense, the first action is expressed in past perfect tense i.e. had + past participle of be (been)

One Word Substitution

One Word Substitution is an essential topic of vocabulary. As the name suggests, questions based on this concept ask you to replace a given sentence with an appropriate word. One word substitution is an important concept in the English language as it makes communication much more concise, lucid, and easy. One-Word Substitution refers to those types of questions where a sentence or a phrase is simply replaced by a word that describes the whole sentence. One-word substitution makes the sentence structure more precise.

Examples

Let's understand One Word Substitution with few examples as below-

- **This person is a hater of mankind:** This person is a misanthrope.

- **Her younger son has an extreme fear of dogs:** Her son has cynophobia.

- **I am interested in the study of ancient things:** I am interested in archaeology.

- **That boy keeps himself very reserved and conservative:** That boy is an introvert.

- **She is someone who puts forth an idea that she herself doesn't believe:** She is a Hypocrite

List of One Word Substitution

The categories of One Word Substitution in English Grammar can be categorized into the following:

1. Study-related
2. Types of Fear

3. Terms-related
4. Group/Collection
5. Likes/Dislikes
6. Government/Political Systems-related
7. People/Person
8. Profession/Occupation
9. Science/Research
10. Killing/Death-related
11. Sound/Event/Spots

Learn One Word Substitution for each category from the below section and enhance your vocabulary skills.

One Word Substitution related to Study

One Word Substitution	Phrases
Aviation	Study of flying aero planes
Astronomy	Study of celestial bodies
Alchemy	The ancient search for a universal panacea, and of the philosopher's stone. The medieval version of the study of Chemistry
Acoustics	Study of sound and sound waves
Anthropology	The study of the evolution of mankind
Astronomy	Study of Stars
Botany	The study of plants
Biology	Study of Living Things
Calligraphy	Art related to ornate, good handwriting
Chronology	The science of time order
Demography	The study of statistics
Entomology	Study of science of insects
Ecology	Study of the relation between the organism and their environment
Genetics	Study of hereditary, genes and variation in living organisms
Geology	The study of rocks and soil
Geography	Mapping of earth and its formation
Graphology	Study of handwriting
Gerontology	Study of various aspects of ageing
Hydraulics	Study of the law of the flow of water and other liquids
Lexicography	The practice of writing dictionaries
Numismatics	Study of collection of coins, tokens, paper money etc.

Ornithology	Study of birds
Philology	The study of languages
Paleography	The study of ancient writing and scriptures
Psychology	The study of Human Mind
Psephology	Study of election trends
Theology	Study of religion

One Word Substitution Related to Types of Fear

One Word Substitution	Phrases
Ecophobia	Fear of home surroundings
Zoophobia	Fear of animals
Claustrophobia	Fear of closed space
Hydrophobia	Fear of Water
Bibliophobia	Fear of books
Xenophobia	Fear or dislike of foreigners
Necrophobia	Fear of dead body
Aerophobia	Fear of height
Ophiophobia	Fear of snakes
Syngenesophobia	Fear of relatives
Nomophobia	Fear of being without your mobile phone

One Word Substitution Related to Killing & Manias

One Word Substitution	Phrase
Mariticide	The killing of one's husband
Parricide	The killing of parents
Genocide	The killing of a whole race
Infanticide	The killing of a newborn child
Regicide	The killing of a king

Homicide	The killing of a human being
Suicide	The killing of oneself
Patricide	The killing of a father
Matricide	The killing of a mother
Fratricide	The killing of one's brother
Sororicide	The killing of one's sister
Uxoricide	The killing of one's wife
Dipsomania	Morbid compulsion to keep on consuming alcohol
Kleptomania	Morbid compulsion to steal
Bibliokleptomania	Morbid compulsion to steal books
Pyromania	Morbid compulsion to start a fire
Megalomania	Morbid delusion of power, importance or godliness
Nymphomania	Morbid, uncontrollable desire on the part of a woman
Satyromaniac	Morbid, uncontrollable desire on the part of a man
Monomania	A person with a one-track mind
Mythomania	The compulsion to tell lies
Mania	Madness with an obsession with something

One Word Substitution Related to Things, Events & Places

One Word Substitution	Phrase
Solarium	A place for the sun to enter where one can sunbath
Aquarium	A glass container in which fish and other water animals can be kept
Podium	A place for feet or a speaker's platform
Auditorium	The part of a theatre where people who are watching and listening sit

Planetarium	An optical device for projecting various celestial images and effects
Sanatorium	An establishment for the treatment of the chronically ill
Museum	A place where objects are exhibited
Deciduous	Trees whose leaves fall every autumn
Incident	That which falls upon befalls happens
Accident	That which falls to someone or something
Occidental	That which falls on the western countries
Alma Mater	The school or college one attends
Automobile	A self-moving vehicle
Automatic	A machine that functions by itself
Perambulator	A baby carriage
Ambulance	A carriage for sick people

One Word Substitution Related to Terms

One Word Substitution	Phrase
Aeon	Indefinite period of time
Aesthetics	Appreciation of beauty, by a set of principles.
Blizzard	Spartan snowstorms with uncontrollable winds
Bohemian	An eccentric manner of living
Bonfire	Huge fire for celebration
Bonsai	Dwarfed varieties of trees and shrubs in pots
Bonfire	Huge fire for celebration
Bonsai	Dwarfed varieties of trees and shrubs in pots
Hinterland	The remote regions of a country which are far away from the rivers

Imbroglio	Complex situation or a mix-up
Rejuvenate	Make someone feel young
Remiss	Not showing enough care and attention
Kennel	A shelter for a Dog
Lair	Where wild animals live:
Mint	A place where coins are made
Mundane	Ordinary and Dull
Posthumous	Published after someone's death
Pedagogy	The profession of teaching or the approach or style of teaching
Regalia	The symbols of royalty
Thearchy	A political system solely based on the government of men by God
Oath	A person promises to tell the truth in court
Nascent	Beginning to exist and evolve
Virtue	Ethically good behaviors one has
Satire	Humor that describes the weaknesses
Veer	Changing the direction of one's path suddenly
Savour	Enjoy something for an extended time
Scapegoat	Someone who is wrongly blamed for things that others have done
Tannery	Space where animal hides are tanned
Tenacious	Determined to achieve something
Screech	The sound of Parrots:
Misnomer	Using a word or name that is inappropriate
Monarchy	A government that has a monarch as the head
Grunt	The sound of Camels

Fiesta	Events manifested by festivities
Whine	The ranting of a person
Destitute	People who are extremely poor
Carte blanche	Absolute freedom to act as one wishes:
Agnostic	A person who is unsure about God's existence:
Agony	Extreme physical or mental sufferings
Aikido	Japanese form of self-defense with the usage of locks holds
Mercenary	A soldier who fights for the sake of money
Laurel	An accolade or honors bestowed in recognition for an achievement:
Immoral	A person who behaves without moral principles
Impeach	Charging a politician with a serious crime
Embargo	Government instructions that limit trade in some way
Fatalist	Believer of fate
Gregarious	Loves being social and enjoys the company of others
Grove	Trees grow without underbrush.
Sinecure	An office with a high salary but no work
Renegade	A person who betrays and descents an organisation or country
Fastidious	One who is much concerned about details and accuracy
Arsenal	A place for storage of arms and ammunition
Excommunicate	One who is expelled from a religious community
Glutton	A person who eats too much
Imitable	Something which can be copied

One Word Substitution Related to People/Person

One Word Substitution	Phrase
Astrophile	A person who is addicted to seeing oneself in mirror
Gastronome	A person who loves food and finds pleasure in eating and drinking
Chromatophilic	A person who loves money
Necrophile	A person who loves dream
Autophile	A person who loves staying single
Melophilia	A person who loves music

One Word Substitution Related to Government

One Word Substitution	Phrase
Bureaucracy	Government by Officials
Autocracy	Government by one person with absolute power
Meritocracy	Government by the intelligentsia
Democracy	Government by elected representatives
Confederacy	The union of states, parties or persons
Plutocracy	Government by rich people
Aristocracy	Government by the nobles
Theocracy	Government by Divine Laws
Monarchy	Government by one person (royal)
Diarchy	Government by two agencies
Oligarchy	Government by a few powerful people
Stratocracy	Government by military class
Anarchy	Absence of Government

One Word Substitution Related to Likes and Dislikes

One Word Substitution	Phrase
Sycophant	One who is a boot licker, flatterer
Gourmet	One who has keen interest in food and drinks
Philanthropy	Love for mankind
Bibliophile	Someone who loves collecting books
Anglophile	One who loves and admires the British
Philanderer	One who loves without seriousness
Philogyny	Fondness towards women
Androphile	One who loves men
Philosopher	One who loves wisdom (hence pursues it)
Misandrist	One who hates men
Andromania	Madness or obsession with males
Misogynist	One who hates women
Misanthropist	One who hates mankind
Patriot	One who loves his country
Super patriotism	Excessive love for one's country
Misogamist	One who hates marriage
Loquacious	One who loves to speak
Antipathy	Strong, deep dislike
Sympathy	Simultaneously affected by similar feelings
Empathy	Mentally identifying oneself with another person or a thing
Pathetic	Something or someone makes you feel deep sadness or pity

One Word Substitution Related to Religion

One Word Substitution	Phrases
Atheist	One who doesn't believe in the presence of God
Monotheist	One who believes in the theory of only one God
Theist	One who believes in the presence of God
Polytheist	One who believes in many Gods
Pantheist	One who believes that God is union of all forces of the universe
Theomania	Religious madness
Theomachy	Battle among the Gods

One Word Substitution Related to Marriage

One Word Substitution	Phrases
Matrimony	Related to marriage
Solo gamy	Marriage with self
Monogamy	Practicing only one marriage (having only one wife)
Bigamy	Practicing two marriages (having two wives)
Polygamy	The practice of several marriages (having many wives)
Autogamy	Self-fertilization especially in plants
Endogamy	Marriage within one's tribe
Exogamy	Marriage outside one's tribe
Polyandry	Having several husbands

One Word Substitution Related to Speech & Written Work

One Word Substitution	Phrase
Omnibus	Book containing all the published work of an author
Telegraph	A written message from far off place
Colloquial	Informal, less grammatically rigid language
Circumlocution	Talking around, a method of talking indirectly
Magniloquent	Generous, forgiving talk
Eloquent	Expressive in the use of words
Grandiloquent	High sounding pompous speech or writing
Autograph	A signature of a celebrity (signature of oneself)
Preamble	Walk before-hand or an introductory statement
Biography	Writing of one's life story
Autobiography	Writing of one's own life story
Photograph	Written by light
Laconic	Few words packed with meaning, concise
Soliloquy	A speech to oneself, alone

MULTIPLE CHOICE QUESTIONS

Direction: In questions given below out of four alternatives, choose the one which can be substituted for the given word/sentence.

1. Open to more than one interpretation; not having one obvious meaning.
A. Trite
B. Opposite
C. Exceptional
D. Ambiguous

Answer: D
Explanation:
Ambiguous means having or expressing more than one possible meaning, sometimes intentionally.

2. Become apparent through the appearance of symptoms.
A. Manifest
B. Distinct
C. Vague
D. Divulged

Answer: A
Explanation:
Manifest means clear or obvious to the eye or mind, Become apparent through the appearance of symptoms.

3. Based on random choice or personal whim.
A. Auxiliary
B. Arbitrary
C. Allegory
D. Ambulatory

Answer: B
Explanation:
Arbitrary based on random choice or personal whim, rather than any reason or system.

4. The recently dead person in question:
A. Obliviate
B. Deceased
C. Euthanized
D. Reposed

Answer: C
Explanation:
Euthanized put an animal to death humanely.

5. Liquids forming a homogenous mixture when added together.
A. Irascible
B. Crucible
C. Miscible
D. Risible

Answer: C
Explanation:
Miscible forming a homogeneous mixture when added together.

6. To delay or prevent someone or something by obstructing them.
A. To perturb
B. To impede
C. To irk
D. To faze

Answer: B
Explanation:
Impede: delay or prevent.

7. To treat with cruelty or violence.
A. Wrong
B. Abuse
C. Pervert
D. Fault

Answer: B
Explanation:
Abuse cruel and violent treatment of a person or animal to use wrongly or improperly; misuse.

8. To pilfer or steal (something, especially an item of small value) in a casual way.
A. To loot
B. To filch
C. To rip off
D. To pluder

Answer: B
Explanation:
Filch means to steal or take surreptitiously in small amounts; pilfer.

9. To have a strong emotional effect on.
A. To smother
B. To yield
C. To overwhelm
D. To forfeit

Answer: C
Explanation:
Overwhelm to have a strong emotional effect on.

10. A substance that has no therapeutic effect, is used as a control in testing new drugs.
A. Sedentary
B. Placebo
C. Lax
D. Torpid

Answer: B
Explanation:
Placebo, A placebo is a substance or treatment with no active therapeutic effect.

11. Feeling or showing deep and solemn respect.
A. Pious
B. Reverent
C. Humble
D. Devout

Answer: D
Explanation:
Devout having or showing deep religious feeling or commitment.

12. Disgusting and an unpleasant smell.
A. Oops
B. Ouch
C. Darn
D. Rancid

Answer: D
Explanation:
Rancid, smelling or tasting unpleasant as a result of being old and stale.

13. A period of time during which a person that might have a disease is kept away from other people so that the disease cannot spread.
A. Solitude
B. Seclusion
C. Quarantine
D. Desolate

Answer: C
Explanation:
Quarantine: A state, period, or place of isolation in which people or animals that have arrived from elsewhere or been exposed to the infectious or contagious disease are placed.

14. To move hurriedly with short quick steps:
A. To scurry
B. To skim
C. To whirl
D. To zip

Answer: A
Explanation:
to move quickly, at a frenzied pace, and often also implies the urge to hide.

15. A person who is not accepted by a social group, especially because he or she is not liked, respected, or trusted
A. Fugitive
B. Vagrant
C. Pariah
D. Tramp

Answer: C
Explanation:
Pariah, a person who is not accepted by a social group, especially because he or she is not liked, respected, or trusted.

16. Having a sensation of whirling and a tendency to fall or stagger.
A. Volatile
B. Wild
C. Reckless
D. Giddy

Answer: D
Explanation:
Giddy, having a sensation of whirling and a tendency to fall or stagger.

17. A rich source of something
A. Antecedent
B. Lode
C. Node
D. Provenience

Answer: B
Explanation:
Lode: a rich source of something.

18. To treat with cruelty or violence
A. Wrong
B. Abuse
C. Pervert
D. Fault

Answer: B
Explanation:
Abuse: cruel and violent treatment of a person or animal.

19. Relating to or characteristic of hell or the underworld
A. Douse
B. Execrable
C. Elysium

D. infernal

Answer: D
Explanation:
Infernal: relating to or characteristics of hell or the underworld.

20. To allay the sorrow or grief
A. To lament
B. To console
C. Distress
D. Solace

Answer: B
Explanation:
Console: to comfort someone at a time of grief or disappointment.

21. Soil deposited by flowing water
A. Humus
B. Clay
C. Loam
D. Alluvium

Answer: D
Explanation:
Alluvium: Clay, silt or gravel carried by rushing streams and deposited where the stream slows down.

22. One who runs away from law
A. Fatalist
B. Convict
C. Fugitive
D. Lunatic

Answer: A
Explanation:
The most appropriate word for the given group of words is Fatalist.
Meaning in English: A person who has escaped from captivity or is in hiding to avoid arrest, prosecution, or punishment.
Example: The police are searching for the fugitive who escaped from prison last week

23. A medicine that soften the bowels
A. Laxative
B. Lexicon
C. Lair
D. Mannequin

Answer: A
Explanation:
Laxative means tending to loosen or relax.
For example- The artificial sweetener sorbitol has a laxative effect.

24. A doctor who specializes in the diseases of the eyes.
A. Cardiologist
B. Ophthalmologist
C. Pathologist
D. Neurologist

Answer: B
Explanation:
Let's have a look at the meaning and example of the marked option:
Ophthalmologist(noun)- "a doctor who treats eye diseases".

25. One for whom money is the most important thing.
A. Matinee
B. Masochist
C. Materialistic
D. Matriarch

Answer: C
Explanation:
Materialistic means believing that having money and possessions is the most important thing in life.
For example- During the 1980s, Britain became a very materialistic society.

26. To walk aimlessly
A. Amble
B. Sprint
C. Crawl
D. Slither

Answer: A
Explanation:
The most appropriate word for the given group of words is 'Amble'.
It means 'to walk at a slow relaxed speed'.
Example: We ambled down to the beach.
27. To throw an event into confusion or disorder
A. Disrupt
B. Detonate
C. Erupt
D. Explode

Answer: A
Explanation:
Let us look into the meaning of the words in the options -
Disrupt - interrupt (an event, activity, or process) by causing a disturbance or problem.

28. Walk or move at a slow, relaxed pace.
A. Amble
B. Romp
C. Strut
D. Prance

Answer: A
Explanation:
The most appropriate word for the given group of words is 'Amble'.
It means 'to walk at a slow relaxed speed'.
Example: We ambled down to the beach.

29. Something that is to your advantage but happened by chance.
A. Occidental
B. Purposeful
C. Deliberate
D. Fortuitous

Answer: D
Explanation:
Fortuitous - happening by chance rather than intention.

30. Something that Pertaining to the controversy
A. Poignancy
B. Laudatory
C. Putative
D. Polemical

Answer: D
Explanation:
The most appropriate word for the given group of words is 'Polemical'.
It means 'of or involving strongly critical or disputatious writing or speech

31. A short stay at a place
A. Voyage
B. Lodge
C. Sojourn
D. Trip

Answer: C
Explanation:
Let us explore the given options:
'Voyage' means a long journey involving travel by sea or in space.
'Lodge' means make or become firmly fixed or embedded in a place.
'Sojourn' means to stay somewhere temporarily.
'Trip' means to go on a short journey.

32. A large bundle bound for storage or transportation
A. Bevy
B. Bouquet
C. Bale
D. Brood

Answer: C
Explanation:
The most appropriate meaning of the given group of words is 'Bale'.
Bale: a large quantity of something pressed tightly together and tied up
Example: When the storm arose on the river, they had to bale out to reach the shore safely.

33. Open refusal to obey orders
A. Obedience

B. Adherence
C. Defiance
D. Compliance

Answer: C
Explanation:
Meaning of the given options are:
Defiance: open resistance; bold disobedience.
Obedience: compliance with an order, request, or law or submission to another's authority.
Adherence: attachment or commitment to a person, cause, or belief.
Compliance: the action or fact of complying with a wish or command.
Thus, defiance is the correct answer.

34. Government by the wealthy
A. Plutocracy
B. Oligarchy
C. Ochlocracy
D. Monarchy

Answer: A
Explanation:
The meanings of the words are:
Plutocracy - Government by the wealthy.
Oligarchy - A small group of people having control of a country or organization.
Ochlocracy - Government by the populace/mob rule.
Monarchy - a form of government with a monarch at the head.

35. A seat for a passenger on a bicycle or motorbike
A. Pillion
B. Girdle
C. Bridle
D. Cushion

Answer: A
Explanation:
Let's see the meanings of the given words-
Pillion- a seat for a passenger behind a motorcyclist.
Girdle- a belt or cord worn around the waist.

Bridle- the headgear used to control a horse, consisting of buckled straps to which a bit and reins are attached.
Cushion- a bag of cloth stuffed with a mass of soft material, used as a comfortable support for sitting or leaning on.

36. A person who renounces the world and practices self-discipline in order to attain salvation:
A. Sceptic
B. Ascetic
C. Devotee
D. Antiquarian

Answer: B
Explanation:
Ascetic: characterized by severe self-discipline and abstention from all forms of indulgence, typically for religious reasons.

37. One who abandons his religious faith:
A. Apostate
B. Prostate
C. Profane
D. Agnostic

Answer: A
Explanation:
Apostate: a person who renounces or abandons a religious or political belief or principle.

38. A hater of knowledge and learning:
A. Bibliophile
B. Philologist
C. Misogynist
D. Misologist

Answer: D
Explanation:
Misologist: A hater of knowledge and learning.

39. Commencement of words with the same letter:
A. Pun

B. Alliteration
C. Transferred epithet.
D. Oxymoron

Answer: B
Explanation:
Alliteration: The occurrence of the same letter or sound at the beginning of adjacent or closely connected words.

40. Person who does not believe in the existence of God:
A. Theist
B. Heretic
C. Atheist
D. Fanatic

Answer: C
Explanation:
Atheist: A person who disbelieves or lacks belief in the existence of God or gods.

41. A lady's umbrella is:
A. Parasol
B. Granary
C. Epitaph
D. Aviary

Answer: A
Explanation:
Parasol: a light umbrella used to give shade from the sun.

42. Story of old-time gods or heroes is:
A. Lyric
B. Epic
C. Legend
D. Romance

Answer: C
Explanation:
Legend: a traditional story sometimes popularly regarded as historical but not authenticated.

43. A sad song
A. Ditty
B. Knell
C. Dirge
D. Lay

Answer: C
Explanation:
Dirge: a mournful song, piece of music, or sound.

44. One who believes in the power of fate:
A. Fatalist
B. Optimist
C. Pessimist
D. Parsimonious

Answer: A
Explanation:
Fatalist: the belief that all events are predetermined and therefore inevitable.

45. A person who loves everybody:
A. Cosmopolitan
B. Fratricide
C. Altruistic
D. Aristocrat

Answer: C
Explanation:
Altruistic: showing a disinterested and selfless concern for the well-being of others; unselfish.

46. A man who rarely speaks the truth:
A. Crook
B. Liar
C. Scoundrel
D. Hypocrite

Answer: B
Explanation:

Liar: a man who rarely speaks the truth

47. A remedy for all diseases
A. Narcotics
B. Antiseptic
C. Panacea
D. Lyric

Answer: C
Explanation:
Panacea: a solution or remedy for all difficulties or diseases.

47. International destruction of racial groups:
A. Matricide
B. Regicide
C. Genocide
D. Homicide

Answer: C
Explanation:
Matricide: the killing of one's mother.
Regicide: the action of killing a king.
Homicide: the killing of one person by another.
Genocide: the deliberate killing of a large group of people, especially those of a particular nation or ethnic group.

48. Custom of having many wives:
A. Misogamy
B. Bigamy
C. Polygamy
D. Monogamy

Answer: C
Explanation:
The one-word substitution is Polygamy.
Misogamy: the hatred of marriage.
Bigamy: the offence of marrying someone while already married to another person.
Monogamy: the practice of marrying or the state of being married to one person at a time.

Polygamy: the practice or custom of having more than one wife or husband at the same time.

49. A pioneer of a reform movement
A. Apostle
B. Apothecary
C. Apotheosis
D. Renegade

Answer: C
Explanation:
The one-word substitution is Apostle.
Apothecary: a person who prepared and sold medicines and drugs.
Apotheosis: the highest point in the development of something; a culmination or climax.
Renegade: a person who deserts and betrays an organization, country, or set of principles.
Apostle: a vigorous and pioneering advocate or supporter of a particular policy, idea, or cause.

50. One who studies insect life
A. Geologist
B. Zoologist
C. Entomologist
D. Botanist

Answer: C
Explanation:
The one-word substitution is Entomologist.
Geologist: one who studies the physical structure and substance of the earth, their history, and the processes which act on them.
Zoologist: one who studies behaviors, structure, physiology, classification, and distribution of animals.
Botanist: one who studies study of the physiology, structure, genetics, ecology, distribution, classification, and economic importance of plants.
Entomologist: One who studies insect life.

Introduction

In 'Fill in the blanks (aka Sentence completion), candidates are given an incomplete sentence with one or more words missing and four options. The candidates are required to choose the right option (word/set of words) to fill the gaps and make the sentence whole.

Read the Given Sentence

Start by reading the given sentence carefully. Understand the crux of the sentence. Try and identify the logical structure of the sentence. This will enable you to determine the kind of word that is required to fill in the blank, based on the context.

Pay Attention to Grammar

You should keep an eye out for grammar hints. Grammatical clues can be extremely useful in determining the correct answer.

Re-read the Sentence

Once you have placed the option in the blank, re-read the sentence. If the sentence makes sense grammatically and logically, it means the word is right.

Elimination

Some sentences have more than one blank. In such cases, you can use the elimination technique to choose the right set of words. Place each set of words in the blanks and eliminate the ones that don't make the sentence complete or don't make it meaningful.

Important Note

- **Read the entire passage:** Before attempting to fill in the blanks, it is important to read the entire passage carefully. This will give you a better understanding of the context and help you to identify which words or phrases might be missing.

- **Look for contextual clues:** Pay attention to the words and phrases that come before and after the blank. These can give you clues about the type of word that is needed to complete the sentence.

- **Identify the part of speech:** Determine what part of speech is needed to fill in the blank. Is it a noun, verb, adjective, or adverb? This will help you to narrow down your choices and select the correct word.

- **Use grammar rules:** Apply grammar rules to the sentence to ensure that the word you choose fits grammatically. For example, if the blank requires a verb, make sure that the tense and subject-verb agreement are correct.

- **Eliminate options:** If you are unsure about which word to choose, eliminate options that are clearly incorrect. This can help you to make an educated guess and increase your chances of getting the answer right.

- **Practice, practice, practice:** The more you practice, the better you will become at identifying the correct words to fill in the blanks. Use practice papers and previous year's question papers to hone your skills and build your confidence.

Functions of Fill in the Blanks

- **Testing understanding and comprehension:** Fill in the blank's questions are often used to test how well a student has understood a concept or idea. By providing a sentence with a missing word, the question is testing whether the student has a clear understanding of the context and can identify the appropriate word to fill in the blank.

- **Assessing vocabulary:** These types of questions are also used to assess a student's vocabulary knowledge. By requiring the student to select the appropriate word from a list of options, the question is testing whether the student has a good understanding of a range of vocabulary.
- **Evaluating grammar and syntax:** Fill in the blank's questions can also be used to evaluate a student's understanding of grammar and syntax. By requiring the student to identify the appropriate part of speech or tense to fill in the blank, the question is testing whether the student has a good grasp of the rules of grammar and how to apply them.

- **Providing feedback:** Fill in the blank's questions can also provide valuable feedback to both the student and the teacher. By identifying areas where the student may be struggling, the teacher can provide targeted support to help the student improve their understanding and skills in that area. Similarly, for the student, the feedback provided by these types of questions can help to identify areas for improvement and guide their study efforts.

Terms of Fill in the Blanks

- **Blank:** The empty space in a sentence or paragraph where a word or phrase is missing, and the student is required to fill in the missing word or phrase.

- **Context:** The words, phrases, and ideas surrounding the blank that provide clues to the student about the type of word or phrase that is needed to fill in the blank.

- **Options:** The list of words or phrases provided to the student from which they must choose the appropriate word or phrase to fill in the blank.

- **Part of speech:** The category of a word (e.g., noun, verb, adjective, adverb, preposition, etc.) that is needed to fill in the blank.

- **Syntax:** The way in which words are arranged to create sentences or phrases. Understanding syntax is important for identifying the correct word to fill in the blank and ensuring that the sentence remains grammatically correct.

- **Tense:** The form of a verb that shows the time at which an action occurred (past, present, future, etc.). Understanding tense is important for selecting the correct verb form to fill in the blank.

Role of Fill in the Blanks

- **Testing understanding and comprehension:** Fill in the blank's questions can help teachers and educators to assess whether students have understood key concepts, ideas, or facts. By providing a sentence with a missing word, these questions can test whether students have comprehended the material and can apply it in a given context.

- **Enhancing vocabulary:** Fill in the blank's questions can help students to expand their vocabulary and improve their word knowledge. By providing a list of options to choose from, these questions can expose students to new words and phrases that they may not have come across before.

- **Improving grammar and syntax:** Fill in the blank's questions can also help students to improve their grammar and syntax skills. By requiring students to identify the correct part of speech or verb tense to fill in the blank, these questions can help students to understand the rules of grammar and syntax and how to apply them correctly.

- **Encouraging critical thinking:** Fill in the blank's questions can also encourage critical thinking skills by requiring students to analyze the context and apply their knowledge to select the correct word or phrase to fill in the blank. This can help students to develop their problem-solving and decision-making skills.

- **Providing feedback:** Fill in the blank's questions can also provide valuable feedback to both students and educators. By identifying areas where students may be struggling or making mistakes, educators can provide targeted support to help students improve their understanding and skills in that area.

Important Role of Fill in the Blanks

Fill in the blank's exercises are an important tool for learning and reinforcing grammar concepts. Here are some reasons why fill in the blanks are important in grammar:

- **Focus on Specific Grammar Concepts:** Fill in the blank's exercises can be tailored to focus on specific grammar concepts, such as verb tenses, prepositions, or articles. This allows learners to practice and reinforce their understanding of those concepts.

- **Encourages Active Learning:** Fill in the blank's exercises require learners to actively engage with the language and apply their knowledge of grammar concepts in context. This encourages learners to think critically about grammar rules and how they are used in real-life situations.

- **Provides Immediate Feedback:** Fill in the blank's exercises provide immediate feedback, allowing learners to correct their mistakes and learn from them. This helps learners to internalize grammar rules and improve their accuracy in using them.

- **Builds Confidence:** Fill in the blank's exercises can help learners build confidence in their ability to use grammar rules correctly. As learners practice and improve their accuracy, they become more confident in their language skills.

- **Versatile Tool:** Fill in the blank's exercises can be used in a variety of ways, such as in classroom activities, homework assignments, or online quizzes. This makes them a versatile tool for language teachers to use in different learning contexts.

Tips to Solve Fill the Blanks Questions

- Knowing general conversational and correct English is the key. Fill in the blanks questions usually don't have very complex sentences and difficult words. They are simple ones but sound in grammar.

- Identifying the common phonetic and spoken English errors can help you master spellings, verb usage, and tenses in a better way.

- Solving fill in the blanks quizzes and practising through sample questions is a good way to improve speed and understanding of this topic.

- Extra reading will always help you master the language and can help your impromptu thinking skills while you attempt the exam.

- Applying the elimination rule while solving each topic of the Fill in the blanks comes very handily.
- In this elimination rule, it requires you to look at the options one after the other and then identify which ones are unsuitable to be used in the blank. Eliminating these options will help you narrow down the choices for the correct option.

- Brushing up vocabulary is an everyday task and can't be done in one day. Keep a habit of reading the newspapers/watching English news/ extra trading to improve your vocabulary.

- Keep practicing grammar exercises. Grammar mistakes are common and need to be rectified if you want to nail the fill in the blanks section.

- Para-jumble exercises are very helpful to give you a clear understanding of sentence structure that also comes in handy while attempting to solve fill in the blanks.

- Time your practice tests. Keep a stopwatch around when you're solving English questions. Yes, you need to think we'll and fill the blank spaces but thinking fast is also important. Hence time management is of prime importance here.

MULTIPLE CHOICE QUESTIONS

1. Fill in the blank: He acted ________ my instructions.
A. Agreeable to
B. According to
C. In favour of
D. In course of

Answer: B
Explanation: Here we use a phrase preposition, according to. The correct statement will be: He acted according to my instructions.

Direction: Read each statement or question below carefully and fill in the blank(s) with the correct answer. Answers may be more than one word.

2. We walked ___ the river and back.
A. Till
B. To
C. At
D. About

Answer: B
Explanation: The preposition used here is- to. Do not use wrong prepositions. To is used with distance and till or until with time.

3. Fill in with appropriate preposition: I have not seen the television ______ yesterday.
A. From
B. Since
C. Till
D. For

Answer: B
Explanation: The correct preposition here would be- since. Since is used before a noun or a phrase, which denotes some point of time. It is preceded by a verb in perfect tense.

4. Today students should be reconciled_______ the way things are changing.
A. With
B. To

C. For
D. At

Answer: B
Explanation:
Today students should be reconciled_______ the way things are changing.

5. The rocket ________the target and did not cause any casualty.
A. sensed
B. reached
C. missed
D. exploded

Answer: C
Explanation:
In this sentence used Preposition. The given sentence talks about a rocket that was fired towards a target.

6. The soldiers received a military ______ to inspect all their vehicles before travelling.
A. allotment
B. dominion
C. affectation
D. mandate

Answer: D
Explanation:
is a command or authoritative instruction.

7. His father _____ him up in a construction business.
A. built
B. hold
C. keep
D. set

Answer: D
Explanation:
SET means to put someone in a particular position.

8. She hadn't eaten all day, and by the time she got home she was ______.

A. blighted
B. confutative
C. ravenous
D. ostentatious

Answer: C
Explanation:
There is a use of Adjective in this sentence.

9. Gita was known to be a ________ so nobody entrusted any important work to her.
A. Joker
B. Worker
C. Shocker
D. Shirker

Answer: D
Explanation:
In the given question, Gita who always evades her work, nobody gives her any important work.

10. What started as a matter of national pride seems to be coming in for ________ from various quarters for a budget that has quadrupled.
A. Shame
B. Feedback
C. Loss
D. Flak

Answer: D
Explanation:
There is a use of Noun in this sentence.

11. We will have to atone ________ our misdeeds.
A. Set
B. On
C. For
D. With

Answer: C

Explanation:
We will have to atone for our misdeeds. The prepositions in and on are mostly used before a noun, pronoun, or noun phrase to show direction, time, place, and location.

12. Each school has its own set of rules ________ all good pupils should follow them
A. But
B. Or
C. So
D. And

Answer: D
Explanation:
and (Conj.) : used for joining words or a group of words or independent clauses without a contrast. Here, and is the right usage.

13. _______politicians are always respected.
A. Conscious
B. Conscientious
C. Cautious
D. Carefree

Answer: B
Explanation:
conscientious (Adj.): taking care to do things carefully and correctly
Here, conscientious is the right usage.

14. It'll rain soon ________ ?
A. Won't it
B. Bought it
C. Isn't It
D. May it

Answer: A
Explanation:
In a positive statement, the question tag is negative. The sentence is in Simple Future Tense
Here, won't it be the right usage.

15. A thorough search of the aircraft was carried ________ in the airport
A. Out

B. Off
C. On
D. Along

Answer: A
Explanation:
carry out (Phr. V.): to do and complete a task. Here, out is the right usage.

16. The traffic also becomes an unfortunate catalyst in ______ the dust particles in the area and around.
A. Collecting
B. Accomplished
C. Combine
D. Dispersing

Answer: D
Explanation:
to spread across or move away over a large area, or to make something do this. In this sentence use Verb.

17. Unchecked garbage burning and fires in open land is ____________Delhi's fight against its deteriorating air quality.
A. Shackled
B. Hiding
C. Spilling
D. Hampering

Answer: D
Explanation:
verb. ham·per ˈham-per. hampered, hampering ˈham-p(ə-)riŋ Synonyms of hamper. transitive verb.

18. The shepherd guarded a large ________ of sheep and allowed them to move from pasture to pasture.
A. Block
B. Culture
C. Shoa
D. Flock

Answer: D

Explanation:

A group of animals (such as birds or sheep) assembled or herded together.

19. The CM _______ citizens of Delhi to join his government to celebrate "Community Diwali" instead of bursting crackers.

A. Requests

B. Attempted

C. Formulated

D. Urged

Answer: D

Explanation:

Is urged a verb or adjective?

verb (used without object), urged, urg·ing.

20. You and your company would be ________ by the standard of both your public and private behaviour.

A. Expected

B. Advanced

C. Judged

D. Enlarged

Answer: C

Explanation:

To form, give, or have as an opinion, or to decide about something or someone, especially after thinking carefully.

21. Seeing his dead father in a movie, the little boy is thrilled because the sight brings his father to him; the mother, on the other hand, finds the scene ________ because it increases her grief hundred-fold.

A. Thrilled

B. Unlike

C. Enthusiastic

D. Unbearable

Answer: D

Explanation:

unbearable/so unpleasant or painful that you find it hard to accept:

22. On my return from a long holiday, I had to ________ with a lot of work

A. Catch on

B. Catch up

C. Make up

D. Take up

Answer: B

Explanation:

Catch up (Verb) % to reach the same level or standard as somebody who is ahead of you. Here, catch up is the right usage.

23. The higher you climb, the more difficult it _____ to breathe.

A. Became

B. Becomes

C. Has become

D. Is becoming

Answer: B

Explanation:

As we go higher from the surface of the Earth, the air in the atmosphere becomes thinner. It becomes difficult to breathe in low oxygen content.

24. The ________ crowd gave the victorious team a tumultuous welcome.

A. Jubilant

B. Troublesome

C. Noisy

D. Arrogant

Answer: A

Explanation:

jubilant (Adjective) : expressing joy

Here, jubiliant is the right usage.

25. Agencies are supposed to transport all ________, suitably covered, to a waste plant, instead of leaving it lying around.

A. Luxury

B. Vehicles

C. Motorcars

D. Debris

Answer: D

Explanation:

The remains of anything broken down or destroyed; ruins; rubble.

26. ________ an old legend King Shirham lived in India.

A. In the event of

B. Due to

C. According to

D. In reference to

Answer: C

Explanation:

According to (Prep.) : as stated or reported by somebody/ something

Here, according to is the right usage.

27. As he got older his belief in these principles did not ________

A. Wither

B. Shake

C. Waver

D. Dither

Answer: A

Explanation:

To sway back & forth, to fluctuate /vary, to tremble, to flatter, to be indecisive.

28. She did not like to ________ her decision like a dictator on her subordinates.

A. Divulge

B. Prompt

C. Enforce

D. Deploy

Answer: C

Explanation:

to make people obey a law, or to make a particular situation happen or be accepted.

29. Criticism that tears down without suggesting areas of improvement is not _____ and should be avoided if possible.

A. Representative

B. Constructive

C. Mandatory

D. Pertinent

Answer: B
Explanation:
Criticism that tears down without suggesting areas of improvement is not constructive and should be avoided if possible.

30. The dean tried to retain control of the situation on the campus, but his attempt was ____ by the board of trustees.
A. Endorsed
B. Frustrated
C. Disclosed
D. Justified

Answer: B
Explanation:
The dean tried to retain control of the situation on the campus, but his attempt was frustrated by the board of trustees.

31. Rita---- her cooking last night.
A. Does not do
B. Did not do
C. Will not do
D. Would not do

Answer: B
Explanation:
Use did not do here because from the use of last night the sentence indicates about the past.

32. I have known her --- the end of the World War II
A. From
B. Since
C. During
D. Toward

Answer: B
Explanation:
Use since because since is used with the present perfect or past perfect tense to denote a

time in the past until a later past time or until now.

33. His appointment may --- some new life into the committee
A. Increase
B. Inject
C. Infect
D. Insure

Answer: A
Explanation:
Use increase here . Increase refers to raise

34. The pages of the book --- by Ravi were lying on the floor.
A. Torn off
B. Torn away
C. Torn of
D. Torn in

Answer: A
Explanation:
Use torn off which refer to separate something by tearing

35. The publisher is bringing ____ a revised edition of this book.
A. Up
B. About
C. Out
D. Round

Answer: C
Explanation:
Bring out means to publish something or to make something appear publicly.

36. She had to ____ Illness in order to avoid going to the party meeting.
A. Fain
B. Feint
C. Feign
D. Faint

Answer: C

Explanation:
Feign means to pretend something.

37. The businessman was very gentle when he mentioned his friends but was bitter and ______ when he discussed people who ____ him.

A. Noisy, encouraged
B. Calm, discouraged
C. Angry, distressed
D. Expressive, disliked

Answer: C
Explanation:
The businessman was very gentle when he mentioned his friends but was bitter and angry when he discussed people who distressed him.

38. Unable to _____ his dislike for the opponent, Mr. Raj continued to make _____ comments through out the meeting.

A. Control, open
B. Express, quiet
C. Disguise, caustic
D. Hide, appreciative

Answer: C
Explanation:
Unable to disguise his dislike for the opponent, Mr. Raj continued to make caustic comments through out the meeting.

39. Nordisk have recently ___________ a product called Glucometer.

A. Started
B. Commissioned
C. Launched
D. Begun

Answer: C
Explanation:
Answer C is correct, because a product is launched. Launch refers to introducing something to the public for the first time. Start means to just begin or set in motion, it is synonymous with begun; whereas, commissioned means to give an official approval.

40. I had already published a novel and it was an unexpected success. I thought my ___________ .

A. Days were up
B. Chances were good
C. Lady luck was happy
D. Fortune was made

Answer: D
Explanation:
The speaker is saying that his novel was a success, but that is not what he/she expected. Option (d) is correct, because making a fortune means achieving a lot of success, prosperity or making lots of money. So, it refers to achieving success, which is what the context is. Option (a) is wrong, because days were up an idiom which refers to ending or coming to an end, this ending could be of anything, like success, happiness etc. But the author, in fact, got success, so this option is logically incorrect. Option (b) is wrong because chances are not talked about after the result and similarly, option (c) can be ruled out too.

Intoduction

English is said to have one of the most difficult spelling systems which people often confuse. The words are misspelt most commonly by the people who use this as a second language, especially, non-natives.

The Indian languages, like Hindi, Bengali or Marathi are based on the stress of the words used and thus the spellings are written on the basis of that. However, the phonetics of English is at times so confusing that the learners often make mistakes. There are basically two reasons for the misspelt words; firstly, the pronunciation of words changes, however, spellings do not. For example, "k" in knife and "yacht" is pronounced as "yot". In the second case, the spelling changes but the pronunciation does not, for example, the word "b" is not pronounced in "doubt". Similarly, words that "ough" like though, bough may sound the same but cough does not.

Learning to avoid using misspelt words

Misspelt words are common in the English language and to avoid this, a dictionary is being used. A dictionary provides a wide range of words alphabetically with the meaning and pronunciation of certain words that are used. However, the English language is very flexible and the pronunciation changes with time. English is a lingua franca and is thus used by the people from all the corners which gradually changes with location. The accent and phonetics changes with each region it travelled. For example, the Indians use English with the influence of Indian words`, and are thus known as "Indian English". The American uses English with different accents and lexicons and is thus known as "American English".

The spellings can be corrected and fixed, if the learner takes the following points into consideration-

- The words should be written neatly and clearly, visualising the words in mind
- The words need to be spelt out loud and pronounced perfectly

- The syllables must be studied carefully and pronounced many times to confirm the usage of words.
- A list must be prepared by the learners for the commonly used words that have often been misspelt.
- Mnemonics or memory aids also help in learning the language using rhymes and word association.
- Commonly misspelt words are generally used unintentionally in general writing. However, there are certain causes that are usually responsible for the commonly misspelt words:
- When the consonants are silent, like, a knife is spelt as "nife"
- Words that break spelling rules, like yacht, is pronounced as "yot"
- Variable spellings in the words ending with the same words, like "donut", are a modern variation of "doughnut".
- Words that are difficult to pronounce, like, rural, squirrel and Otorhinolaryngologist.
- Immediately Repeated Syllable Spellings, like, Quarantine
- English is a flexible language with variety and the language is used by almost all countries to communicate in their national and international situations. Learners often commit mistakes and learn from the same mistakes using misspelt words. The correct practice of pronunciation, learning spellings and grammar helps them to enhance the learning of the spellings.

List of commonly used words that are misspelled.

Common misspelt words	Correct spelling
Acceptible	Acceptable
Acheive	Achieve
Aknolege	Acknowledge
Ackwantance	Acquaintance
Accquire	Acquire
Artic	Arctic
Begining	Beginning
Capitle	Capital
Dissapoint	Disappoint

Estreme	Extreme
Fassinating	Fascinating
Immitate	Imitate
Medival	Medieval
Profesor	Professor
Refered	Referred
Surprize	Surprise
Thier	Their
Writting	Writing
Definitely	Defiantly
Caribbean	Carribean
Separate	Seperate
Humorous	Humerous
Guarantee	Garanty
Until	Untill
Occasionally	Occassionally
Immediately	Imediately
Questionnaire	Questionnair

The table given above presents the commonly used words that are misspelt. Apart from these, some common mistakes occur with the following circumstances-

- Words ending with ar, er, or orre: beggar, borrower, theatre.
- Words ending with al, el, le: Annual, Signal, Musical
- Words ending with ur, ure, eur, our: Assure, Architecture, Rigour, Sulphur
- Words ending with ry, ary,, ery, ory: Dowry, Bakery, Surgery
- Words ending with ance, ence, ense: Acceptance, Defence, Influence, Presence
- Words ending with able, ible: Advisable, Vegetable, Flexible, Sensible
- Words ending with cial, tial: official, substantial, initial, session, station
- Troublesome words: Accommodate, Beggar, Career, Ceremony, Behavior, Naughty, Goddess, Hungry, Tuition, Pursue, Harass, Height, Ancient

Sometimes the words sound the same but they are different in different spellings with different meanings. However, many times there are certain words that are often confused by the other words. Apart from this, many at times, the same words have different meanings and are thus being confused by the learners to use it correctly and properly. These are the general problems that students face during their learning phase. These mistakes are also made by adults, even those who are experienced in certain fields of education. The commonly misspelt words are a common mistake that may change the meaning of the Centre along with an error in the construction and structure.

MULTIPLE CHOICE QUESTION

1. Select the wrongly spelt word.
A. Fixation
B. Providance
C. Musician
D. Consequence

Answer: B.
Explanation:
Providance has the wrongly spelt word. The correct spelling of the word is 'providence' which means an influence that is not human in origin and is thought to control people's lives. Other words and their meanings are:
Fixation means the state of being unable to stop thinking about something or someone, or an unnaturally strong interest in something or someone.
A musician means someone who is skilled in playing music, usually as a job. Consequence means a result of a particular action or situation, often one that is bad or not convenient. Circumstance means a condition or fact that affects a situation.

2. Select the wrongly spelt word.
A. Mimic
B. Subtle
C. Esteem
D. Respectfull

Answer: D
Explanation:
Respectfull has the wrongly spelt word. The correct spelling of the word is 'respectful' which means showing admiration for someone or something.
Other words and their meanings are: Mimic means to copy the way in which a particular person usually speaks and moves, usually in order to make people laugh.
Subtle means not loud, bright, noticeable, or obvious in any way. Esteem means respect for or a good opinion of someone.

3. Select the word with the incorrect spelling.
A. Denounce
B. Ascertain
C. Systemetic

D. Combination

Answer: C

Explanation:

Systemetic has the incorrectly spelt word. Its correct spelling is 'systematic' which means something 'done or acting according to a fixed plan or system'. Other words and their meanings are: Denounce means to criticize something or someone strongly and publicly. The combination means the mixture you get when two or more things are combined. Ascertain means to discover something. Comfortable means allowing you to be relaxed, causing no worries, difficulty, or uncertainty.

4. Select the word with the correct spelling.

A. Impresionable

B. Propencity

C. Systamatic

D. Impeccable

Answer: D

Explanation:

Impeccable has the correctly spelt word. It means without any mistakes or faults, perfect. Other words with their correct spellings and meanings: Impressionable means easily influenced. Propensity means a habit of behaving in a particular way. Susceptible means are likely or liable to be influenced or harmed by a particular thing. Splendid means are magnificent, very impressive.

5. Select the word with the incorrect spelling.

A. Medetative

B. Appended

C. Apprehensive

D. Pensive

Answer: A

Explanation:

Medetative has the incorrectly spelt word and the correct spelling is Meditative which means involving meditation (concentrating on one thing). Other words and their meanings are: Appended means add something to the end of a written document. Apprehensive means worried. Pensive means engaged in serious thought

6. Select the wrongly spelt word.
A. Manifestation
B. Manipulation
C. Eradication
D. Regularization

Answer: A
Explanation:
Manifestation has the wrongly spelt word. Manifestation is the correct spelling of the word. It means a sign that something is happening. Other words and their meanings are Manipulation means controlling someone or something to your own advantage, often unfairly or dishonestly. Eradication means the process of getting rid of something completely or of destroying something bad. Regularization means the act of changing a situation or system so that it follows laws or rules or is based on reason. Ludicrous means laughable through obvious absurdity.

7. Select the wrongly spelt word.
A. Representative
B. Palliative
C. Lucretive
D. Productive

Answer: C
Explanation:
Lucretive has the wrongly spelt word. The correct spelling of the word is 'lucrative'. It means allowing somebody to earn a lot of money. Other words and their meanings are:
A representative means someone who speaks or does something officially for another person or group of people. Palliative means (of a drug or medical treatment) reducing pain without curing the cause of the pain. Productive means resulting in or providing a large amount or supply of something. Permeate means to pass or spread through (something).

8. Select the wrongly spelt word.
A. Telepathy
B. Allopathy
C. Naturopathy
D. Homoepathy

Answer: D

Explanation:

Homoepathy has the wrongly spelt word. The correct spelling is 'homeopathy' and it is a pseudoscientific system of alternative medicine. Other words and their meanings are: Telepathy means the purported vicarious transmission of information from one person to another without using any known human sensory channels or physical interaction.

Allopathy means the treatment of disease by conventional means, i.e., with drugs having effects opposite to the symptoms. Naturopathy means a system of health care that promotes the body's own self-healing mechanism. Medicine means the science of preventing and treating illness.

9. Find the correctly spelt word.

A. Conspicuous

B. Persistence

C. Renaissance

D. Thesaurus

Answer: D

Explanation:

The correctly spelt word is a thesaurus which means a book that contains lists of words and phrases with similar meanings. The correct spellings of the other words are persistence, conspicuous, renaissance.

10. Select the word with the incorrect spelling.

A. Quantity

B. Argument

C. Quarrell

D. Aisle

Answer: C

Explanation:

Quarrell has the wrongly spelt word. The correct spelling is "quarrel" and it means an angry argument or disagreement. Other words and their meanings are Quantity means a number or an amount of something. Argument means an angry discussion between two or more people who disagree with each other. Aisle means a passage between the rows of seats in a church, theatre, etc. Decongestant means medicine that helps stop thick fluid from building up in your nose, throat, or chest when you have a cold or similar illness.

11. Select the incorrectly spelt word.
A. Abbreviate
B. Accommodate
C. Admittance
D. Aggresser

Answer: D
Explanation:
Aggresser has the wrongly spelt word. The correct spelling is "aggressor" which means a person or country that attacks another first. Meaning of other words are: - Abbreviate means to shorten (a word, phrase, or text). Accommodation means providing lodging or sufficient space for. Admittance means the process or fact of entering or being allowed to enter a place or institution.

12. Select the incorrectly spelt word.
A. Squall
B. Idyll
C. Skelful
D. Shameful

Answer: C
Explanation:
Skelful has the wrongly spelt word. The correct spelling is 'skillful' which means having or showing skill. Meaning of other words are Squall means a sudden violent gust of wind or localized storm, especially one bringing rain, snow, or sleet. Idyll means an extremely happy, peaceful, or picturesque period or situation, typically an idealized or unsustainable one. Shameful means worthy of or causing shame or disgrace. Tactful means are careful not to offend or upset other people, having or showing tact.

13. Select the correctly spelt word.
A. Monopolly
B. Monapoly
C. Monnopoly
D. Monopoly

Answer: D
Explanation:
Monopoly has the correctly spelt word which means exclusive control, possession or use of something.

14. Select the correctly spelt word.
A. Commemorete
B. Comemorate
C. Commemmorate
D. Commemorate

Answer: D
Explanation:
The correctly spelt word is Commemorate. "Commemorate" means to organize or do something in memory of a past event.

15. Select the correctly spelt word.
A. Hoseire
B. Hosier
C. Hosair
D. Hasier

Answer: B
Explanation:
Hosier has the correctly spelt word. "Hosier" means a manufacturer or seller of hosiery (stockings, socks, and tights collectively).

16. Select the incorrectly spelt word.
A. Deliquescence
B. Pertinacious
C. Pisiculture
D. Renaissance

Answer: C
Explanation:
Pisiculture has the incorrectly spelt word. The correct spelling is pisciculture. Pisciculture involves raising fish commercially in tanks or enclosures such as fish ponds, usually for food. The meanings of the other words are: Deliquescence means tending to melt or dissolve especially. Pertinacious means holding firmly to an opinion or a course of action. Renaissance means a new growth of activity or interest in something, especially art, literature, or music. Renegade means someone or something that causes trouble and cannot be controlled.

17. Select the incorrectly spelt word.
A. Millennium
B. Millionaire
C. Millenerian
D. Manageable

Answer: C
Explanation:
Millenerian has the wrongly spelt word. The correct spelling is millenarian. It is a belief in Christian millenarianism. The meaning of the other words are Millennium means a period of a thousand years, especially when calculated from the traditional date of the birth of Christ. A millionaire means a person whose assets are worth one million pounds or dollars or more. Manageable means are able to be controlled or dealt with without difficulty.

18. Four words are given, out of which only one word is spelt correctly?
A. Dysorientation
B. Desorientation
C. Disorientation
D. Disorientetion

Answer: C
Explanation:
The correctly spelt word is disorientation means a feeling of being confused about where you are, where you are going, or what is happening.

19. Choose the correctly spelt word.
A. Monotheeism
B. Misogynist
C. Morotorium
D. Momentery

Answer: B
Explanation:
The correctly spelt word is misogynist means a man who hates women. The correct spellings of the other words are momentary, monotheism, moratorium.

20. Select the wrongly spelt word.
A. Cautiously
B. Consequantly

C. Completely
D. Concurrently

Answer: B
Explanation:
Consequantly is the wrongly spelt word. The correct spelling is 'Consequently' which means accordingly. Cautiously means careful. Completely means totally or utterly. Concurrently means occurring at the same time, simultaneously.

21. Select the Incorrectly spelt word.
A. Delicious
B. Journy
C. Furious
D. Failure

Answer: B
Explanation:
Journy has the incorrectly spelt word. The correct word is a journey which refers to the act of travelling from one place to another. Meaning of other words: delicious means greatly pleasing or entertaining. Furious means marked by extreme and violent energy. Failure means an event that does not accomplish its intended purpose. Ruthless means having no pity, cruel or merciless.

22. Select the Incorrectly spelt word.
A. Affiliate
B. Annihilate
C. Exclaimation
D. Aesthetic

Answer: C
Explanation:
The incorrectly spelt word is "Exclaimation" and the correct spelling is "Exclamation" which means a sudden cry or remark expressing pleasure, surprise, agreement, etc. Let's understand the meaning of other words: Affiliate means a person or organization officially attached to a larger body. Annihilate means to destroy/defeat somebody/something completely. Aesthetic means concerned with beauty or art. Artificial means not genuine or natural but made by people.

23. Select the Incorrectly spelt word.
A. Hurdle
B. Cuddel
C. Puddle
D. Meddle

Answer: B
Explanation:
Cuddel has the incorrectly spelt word. Its correct spelling is 'cuddle' which means hold close in one's arms as a way of showing love or affection. The meanings of the other words are: Hurdle means a problem, difficulty, or part of a process that may prevent you from achieving something. A puddle means a small pool of liquid, especially rainwater on the ground. Meddle means to interfere in something that is not one's concern. Middle means the part, point, or position that is at about the same distance from the two ends or sides of something.

24. Select the correctly spelt word.
A. Agression
B. Temprature
C. Millionare
D. Catalogue

Answer: D
Explanation:
The correctly spelt word is "Catalogue" which means a complete list of things that you can look at, buy or use. Let's see the spellings and meanings of other words: Aggression means a feeling of anger resulting in violent behavior. Temperature means the intensity of heat present in an object. A millionaire means a person who has a million pounds, dollars, etc.

25. Select the correctly spelt word.
A. Beaureacracy
B. Reimbursement
C. Surveliance
D. Recrutment

Answer: B
Explanation:
Reimbursement has the correctly spelled word. Reimbursement means compensation paid (to someone) for damages, losses or money already spent, etc. Correct spelling of other

words along with their meanings: Bureaucracy means a government that is administered primarily by bureaus that are staffed with nonselective officials. Surveillance means to close the observation of a person or group (usually by the police). Recruitment means the act of getting recruits; enlisting people for the army (or for a job or a cause etc.). Reduce means to make something less or smaller in quantity, price, size, etc.

26. Select the wrongly spelt word.
A. Machenic
B. Medieval
C. Magazine
D. Measure

Answer: A
Explanation:
The wrongly spelt word is Machenic. The correct spelling is mechanic which corresponds to a skilled worker who repairs and maintains vehicle engines and other machinery. Medieval means relating to, or characteristic of the Middle Ages. Magazine means a print periodical containing miscellaneous pieces (such as articles, stories, poems) and often illustrated. The measure means an adequate or due portion. Meditation means the act or process of meditating.

27. Select the wrongly spelt word.
A. Latitude
B. Latter
C. Lateral
D. Lathargy

Answer: D
Explanation:
Lathargy has the wrongly spelt word. The correct spelling is 'Lethargy', which means lack of enthusiasm or energy. Latitude means a region or locality as marked by its latitude. Latter means belonging to a subsequent time or period. Lateral means situated on, directed toward, or coming from the side.

28. Four words are given, out of which only one word is spelt correctly. Choose the correctly spelt word.
A. Counterfeit
B. Counterfeet
C. Counterfit

D. Counterfiet

Answer: A
Explanation:
The correctly spelt word is counterfeit. Counterfeit means made in exact imitation of something valuable, fake, forged.

29. Select the correctly spelt word.
A. Defnition
B. Acceptence
C. Scramble
D. Jewlry

Answer: C
Explanation:
'Scramble' meaning 'make one's way quickly or awkwardly up a steep gradient or over rough ground by using one's hands as well as one's feet' is the correctly spelt word.

30. Select the correctly spelt word.
A. Cleaver
B. Sentiment
C. Taelant
D. Serenity

Answer: D
Explanation:
Serenity has the correctly spelt word. 'Serenity' meaning 'the state of being calm, peaceful, and untroubled'. The correct spelling of other words along with their meanings: Clever means mentally quick and resourceful. The sentiment means tender, romantic, or nostalgic feeling or emotion. Talent means a person who possesses unusual innate ability in some field or activity.

31. Select the incorrectly spelt word.
A. Convenience
B. Customary
C. Coveteus
D. Counsellor

Answer: C

Explanation:
Coveteus has the incorrectly spelt word. Covetous means having or showing a great desire to possess something belonging to someone else. The meaning of the other words are:- Convenience means the state of being able to proceed with something without difficulty. Customary means according to the customs or usual practices associated with a particular society, place, or set of circumstances. Counsellor means a person trained to give guidance on personal or psychological problems.

32. Select the correctly spelt word.
A. Dievorce
B. Carapase
C. Usefully
D. Shuffels

Answer: D
Explanation:
Usefully has the correctly spelt word i.e., 'usefully' which means in a useful manner. The correct spellings of the other words along with their meanings are:- Divorce means the legal dissolution of a marriage by a court or other competent body. Carapace means the hard upper shell of a tortoise, crustacean, or arachnid. Shuffle means to mix and jumble.

33. Select the correctly spelt word.
A. Infetuote
B. Horrandeous
C. Ricuresion
D. Precarious

Answer: D
Explanation:
Precarious has the correctly spelt word i.e., 'precarious' which means 'affording no ease or reassurance'. Infatuation means arouse unreasoning love or passion in and cause to behave in an irrational way. Horrendous means causing fear, dread or terror. Recursion means calling a function from within the same function.

34. Select the correctly spelt word.
A. Sanguine
B. Sanquin
C. Sankuine
D. Precarious

Answer: A
Explanation:
The correctly spelt word is sanguine means cheerful, hopeful and confident about the future.

35. Select the incorrectly spelt word.
A. Inefficent
B. Independence
C. Influence
D. Inequality

Answer: A
Explanation:
Inefficent has the wrongly spelt word. The correct word is inefficient which means lacking skills. Independence means freedom. Influence means charm or temptation. Inequality means lacking equality.

36. Select the incorrectly spelt word.
A. Admiration
B. Adreneline
C. Adroit
D. Administration

Answer: B
Explanation:
Adreneline has the incorrectly spelt word. The correct spelling is Adrenaline which is a stress hormone. Meaning of other words are: - Admiration means warm approval. Adroit means skillful. Administration means management.

37. Select the incorrectly spelt word.
A. Dreamy
B. Dreadful
C. Dribble
D. Drougth

Answer: D
Explanation:
Drougth has the wrongly spelt word. The correct spelling is Drought means a shortage of rainfall. Dreamy means lacking spirit or liveliness. Dreadful means alarming or extremely bad. Dribble means run or flow slowly in the form of drops.

38. Select the incorrectly spelt word.
A. Laboriaus
B. Mysterious
C. Courteous
D. Religious

Answer: A
Explanation:
Laboriaus has the incorrectly spelt word. The correct spelling is "laborious" which means effortful or arduous, an effort to the point of exhaustion. Other words and their meanings are: Mysterious means are incomprehensible or inexplicable. Courteous means gallant, respectful and gracious. Religious means spiritual or scrupulous.

39. Select the incorrectly spelt word.
A. Dungeon
B. Dillapidated
C. Demonstrate
D. Religious

Answer: B
Explanation:
Dillapidated has incorrectly spelt word. The correct spelling is "dilapidated" which means old and in poor condition. The meaning of the other words are as follows: Dungeon means a strong underground prison cell, especially in a castle. Demonstrate means clearly showing the existence or truth of (something) by giving proof orevidence.

40. Select the incorrectly spelt word.
A. Curriculum
B. Couregeous
C. Collaborate
D. Cylinder

Answer: B
Explanation:
Couregeous has the incorrectly spelt word. Its correct spelling is "courageous" which means not deterred by danger or pain; brave. The meanings of the other words are: Curriculum means the subjects comprising a course of study in a school or college. Collaborate means working jointly on an activity or project. A cylinder means a solid or hollow tube with long

straight sides and two circular ends the same size, or an object shaped like this, often used as a container.

41. Select the correctly spelt word.
A. Flurocent
B. Fragrent
C. Flamboyant
D. Fragmant

Answer: B
Explanation:
The correctly spelt word is flamboyant which means (used about a person) acting in a loud, confident way that attracts attention. The correct spellings of the other words are:- Fragrant means having a pleasant smell. Fragment means a small piece that has broken off or that comes from something larger. Fluorescent means producing a bright white light by radiation.

42. Select the wrongly spelt word.
A. Avertion
B. Omission
C. Aviation
D. Evasion

Answer: A
Explanation:
Avertion has the wrongly spelt word. The correct spelling is "aversion" which means "a strong dislike". Meaning of other words: - Omission means removal. Aviation means air transport. Evasion means to avoid.

43. Choose the Misspelt word.
A. Perseverance
B. Possession
C. Reference
D. Restarant

Answer: D
Explanation:
'Restaurant' meaning 'a place where people pay to sit and eat meals that are cooked and served on the premises' is incorrectly spelt as 'restarant'. Perseverance means continued

effort to do or achieve something despite difficulties, failure, or opposition. Possession means the state of having or owning something. Reference means a written or spoken comment that mentions somebody/something.

44. Select the correctly spelt word.
A. Benigne
B. Bennine
C. Benine
D. Benign

Answer: D
Explanation:
Benign has the correctly spelt word. The meaning of 'benign' is 'friendly or not harmful in effect'.

45. Select the correctly spelt word.
A. Creddible
B. Credibal
C. Credibel
D. Credible

Answer: D
Explanation:
The correct spelling is 'credible'. Credible means 'which/who is worthy of being trusted/believed'.

46. Select the correctly spelt word.
A. Unweded
B. Informmer
C. Mongrels
D. Powderred

Answer: C
Explanation:
Mongrels have the correctly spelt word. It means a dog of no definable type or breed. Other words with their correct spellings and meanings are: Unwedded means not married. Informer means the person who informs another person to the police or other authority. Powdered means in the form of powder. Palate means the roof of the mouth separating the mouth from the nasal cavity.

47. Select the correctly spelt word.
A. Haunchhes
B. Exulltant
C. Marketted
D. Transmit

Answer: D
Explanation:
Transmit means to cause (something) to pass on from one person or place to another. Other words with their correct spelling and meanings are: Haunches mean a buttock and thigh considered together, in a human or animal. Exultant means triumphantly happy. Marketed means to advertise or promote (something).

48. Select the correctly spelt word.
A. Meriteocratic
B. Meritocratik
C. Meritocretik
D. Meritocratic

Answer: D
Explanation:
Meritocratic has the correctly spelt word. Meritocratic means the characteristic of society where power is held by people chosen by their merit.

49. Select the incorrectly spelt word.
A. Reproduce
B. Reverse
C. Require
D. Resembel

Answer: D
Explanation:
Resembel has the wrongly spelt word. The correct word is 'resembled' which means appear alike or similar. Reproduce means make a copy of. Reverse means contrary or opposite. Require means necessitate.

50. Select the incorrectly spelt word.
A. Nerve
B. Neglect

C. Negative
D. Nerveous

Answer: D
Explanation:
Nerveous has the wrongly spelt word. The correct word is 'nervous' which means marked by anxiety. Nerve means a nerve is an enclosed, cable-like bundle of nerve fibers called axons, in the peripheral nervous system. Neglect means to show no concern. Negative means bad or harmful. Natural means are based on an inherent sense of right and wrong.

VOICE

Introduction

Voice is that form of the transitive verb that shows whether the subject of the sentence is the doer of the action or has the action done to it.

For example: 'Mohan played football.'

This sentence is said to be in the active voice. Here, Mohan is the subject and he is the doer of the action, i.e. 'played football'. The action of the subject is transferred to the object 'football' because Mohan has done something to the 'football'.

The passive voice of this sentence is:

Football was played by Mohan.

Here the subject is 'football' which was 'object' in the active sentence. So here something is done to the subject 'football', i.e. it suffers the action done by something or someone.

Rules for the Change of Voice

The object of the active sentence becomes the subject of the verb in the passive voice. The preposition 'by' is put before it.

The main verb of the active sentence changes into the past participle.

The form of the verb to be am, is, are, was, were, being, been is placed before the main verb according to the tense.

The auxiliary verb is changed according to the new subject in number and person.

Changes in Pronouns

Active Voice Subjective case		Passive Voice Objective case
I	→	by me
We	→	by us
You	→	by you
He	→	by him
She	→	by her

It	→	by it
They	→	by them

Change in tenses from Active Voice to Passive Voice

Tense/Aspect	Active voice	Passive Voice
Simple Present	He kills a snake.	A snake is killed by him.
Simple Past	He killed a snake.	A snake was killed by him
Simple Future	She will write a letter.	A letter will be written by her.
Present Progressive	She is singing a song.	A song is being sung by her.
Past Progressive	She was singing a song.	A song was being sung by her.
Present Perfect	They have watered the plants.	The plants have been watered by them.
Past Perfect	We had helped him.	He had been helped by us.
Future Perfect	I will have beaten him.	He will have been beaten by me.

Change of Voice in the Simple Present

Active voice	Passive voice
1. He reads a novel.	A novel is read by him.
2. He does not obey his teachers.	His teachers are not obeyed by him.
3. Why do you waste time?	Why is time wasted by you?
4. Who teaches you Physics?	By whom are you taught Physics?
5. Which book do you read these days?	Which book is read by you these days?

Past Simple Tense

Active voice	Passive voice

1. He did not help me.	I was not helped by him.
2. I told her a story.	A story was told to her by me.
3. What did she buy?	What was bought by her?
4. Whom did you meet?	Who was met by you?
5. Did you read this novel?	Was this novel read by you?

Simple Future

Active voice	Passive voice
1. I shall help him.	He will be helped by me.
2. Will you sell this house?	Will this house be sold by you?
3. Who will pay the bill?	By whom will the bill be paid?
4. You will not disturb me.	I shall not be disturbed by you.
5. When will you visit us?	When shall we be visited by you?

Types of Voice

1. **Active Voice**
2. **Passive Voice**

Understanding the Types of Voices

Now, examine the following sentences carefully.

- Raghav sold his old car. Active voice
- His old car was sold by Raghav. Passive voice

Q. What is the action being performed in both sentences?
Selling = Verb
Q. Who is selling?
Raghav = Subject
Q. What is being sold?
Old car = Object

- No matter whether the sentence begins with 'Raghav' or 'His old car', the performer of the action of selling is 'Raghav'. Therefore 'Raghav' is the subject.

- And the sentence beginning with the subject 'Raghav' i.e., Raghav sold his old car, is in active voice whereas the sentence beginning with 'His old car', the receiver of the action object i.e. His old car was sold by Raghav is in passive voice.
- So, now, it is crystal clear that if you understand who the performer of the action is, it becomes very easy to decide whether the sentence you want to form will follow the syntax of Active or Passive voice.
- **Active Voice:** A **verb** is said to be in the Active Voice when the person or thing denoted by the subject is the doer of the action **when the subject acts or is active.**
- **Passive Voice:** A **verb** is said to be in the Passive Voice when the person or thing denoted by the subject is the receiver of the action **when the subject is passive/acted upon.**

Change of Voice

While changing a verb from Active voice to Passive voice, the following general rules should be followed:

1. The object of the active verb is made the subject of 'the passive verb.
2. The subject of the active verb is made the object of the passive verb. This object is preceded by a preposition mostly 'by'; in some cases, 'to' or 'with'. It will be elucidated further in the chapter.
3. The passive voice must contain the third form of the main or finite verb.
4. Helping verb is placed before the main verb.
5. The form of the verb is changed according to the tense.

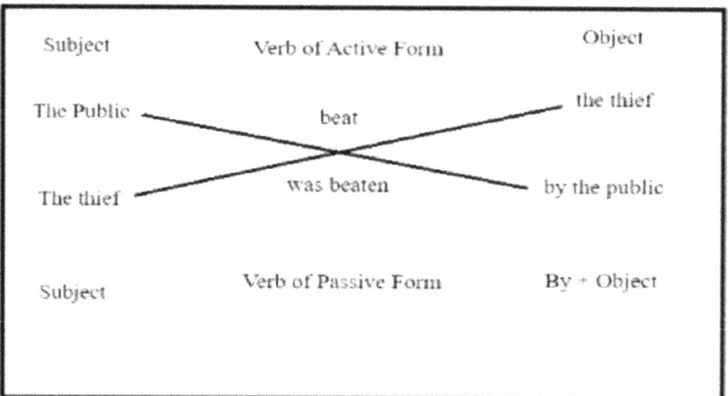

1. Present Tense

1. Simple Present Tense

Active: S + V1 first form of verb + O

Passive: 'O' + am/is/are + V3 third form of verb + by + 'S'

Examples:

- I baked a cake today. **Active voice**
  A cake was baked by me today. **Passive voice**
- NDTV launches gadgets360.com soon. **Active voice**
  Gadgets360.com will be launched soon by NDTV. **Passive voice**
- The jury will declare the results in a few minutes. **Active voice**
  The results will be declared in a few minutes by the jury. **Passive voice**
- Anushka and Neha learn Salsa. **Active voice**
  Salsa is learnt by Anushka and Neha. **Passive voice**
- Archaeologists study the fossils. **Active voice**
  The fossils are studied by archaeologists. **Passive voice**

2. Present Continuous Tense

Active: S + am/is/are + V1 + ing + O

Passive: O + am/is/are + being + V3 + by + S

Examples:

- Rishabh is painting the portrait of a lady. **Active voice**
  The portrait of a lady is being painted by Rishabh. **Passive voice**
- The police are investigating the matter. **Active voice**
  The matter is being investigated by the police. **Passive voice**
- She is preparing the list of guests for the party. **Active voice**
  The list of guests for the party is being prepared by her. **Passive voice**
- Indian scientists are developing the technology against data hacking. **Active voice**
  The technology against data hacking is being developed by Indian scientists. **Passive voice**
- The secretary of the manager is preparing the agenda of the meeting. **Active voice**
  The agenda of the meeting is being prepared by the secretary of the manager. **Passive voice**

3. Present Perfect Tense

Active: S + has/have + V3 + O

Passive: O + has/have + been + V3 + by + S

Examples:

- Ovi has changed the channel on TV. **Active voice**
  The channel on TV has been changed by Ovi. **Passive voice**
- Anurag Basu has made a few very good movies. **Active voice**
  A few very good movies have been made by Anurag Basu. **Passive voice**
- They have auctioned ‘Shabnam Villa’. **Active voice**

‘Shabnam Villa’ has been auctioned by them. **Passive voice**

- Nitika and Vihaan have revealed their secrets. **Active voice**
  Their secrets have been revealed by Nitika and Vihaan. **Passive voice**
- This book has incorporated all the important topics. **Active voice**
  All the important topics have been incorporated by this book. **Passive voice**

2. Past Tense

1. Simple Past Tense
Active: S + V2 + O
Passive: O + was/were + V3 + by + S
Examples:

- We submitted the assignments last week. **Active voice**
  The assignments were submitted last week by us. **Passive voice**
- Sakshi cracked GRE at the very first attempt. **Active voice**
  GRE was cracked at the very first attempt by Sakshi. **Passive voice**
- India won last Hockey World Cup many years back. **Active voice**
  Last Hockey World Cup was won many years back by India. **Passive voice**
- Vansh grabbed four prizes at the Inter School competitions. **Active voice**
  Four prizes were grabbed by Vansh at the Inter-school competition. **Passive voice**
- My father purchased this car in the year 1997. **Active voice**
  This car was purchased in the year 1997 by my father. **Passive voice**

2. Past Continuous Tense
Active: S + was/were + V1 + ing + O
Passive: O + was/were + being + V3 + by + S
Examples

- He was practising Hinduism. **Active voice**
  Hinduism was being practised by him. **Passive voice**
- Sumi was counting stars in the sky. **Active voice**
  Stars in the sky were being counted by Sumi. **Passive voice**
- They were flying kites. **Active voice**
  Kites were being flown by them. **Passive voice**
- Sejal and Mahima were planting trees in the garden. **Active voice**
  Trees were being planted in the garden by Sejal and Mahima. **Passive voice**
- Radha was searching for something in the cupboard. **Active voice**

Something was being searched in the cupboard by Radha. **Passive voice**

3. Past Perfect Tense
Active: S + had + V3 + O
Passive: O + had been + V3 + by + S
Examples:

- I had already done this. **Active voice**
  This had been already / had already been done by me. **Passive voice**
- He had tolerated much before coming to this city. **Active voice**
  Much had been tolerated by him before coming to this city. **Passive voice**
- Sahil had sent the invitation letter. **Active voice**
  The invitation letter had been sent by Sahil. **Passive voice**
- Noorjahan had learnt many recipes of Chinese food. **Active voice**
  Many recipes of Chinese food had been learnt by Noorjahan. **Passive voice**
- Rudra had not accepted the offer. **Active voice**
  The offer had not been accepted by Rudra. **Passive voice**

3. Future Tense

1. Simple Future Tense
Active: S + shall/will + V1 + O
Passive: O + shall/will + be + V3 + by + S
Examples:

- He will manipulate her. **Active voice**
  She will be manipulated by him. **Passive voice**
- We will find out a solution. **Active voice**
  A solution will be found out by us. **Passive voice**
- Trespassers shall not use this road. **Active voice**
  This road shall not be used by trespassers. **Passive voice**
- God will endow him with the power of speech one day. **Active voice**
  He will be endowed with the power of speech by God one day. **Passive voice**
- The boss will not entertain his lame excuses. **Active voice**
  His lame excuses will not be entertained by the boss. **Passive voice**

2. Future Perfect Tense
Active: S + shall/will have + V3 + O

Passive: O + shall/will have + been + V3 + by + S

Examples:

- Mother will have prepared a delicious lunch. **Active voice**
  Delicious lunch will have been prepared by mother. **Passive voice**
- You will have won the game. **Active voice**
  The game will have been won by you. **Passive voice**
- India will have eradicated illiteracy by 2020. **Active voice**
  Illiteracy will have been eradicated by 2020 by India. **Passive voice**
- Shanu will have eaten up all the chocolates. **Active voice**
  All the chocolates will have been eaten up by Shanu. **Passive voice**
- Miheer will have surprised her. **Active voice**
  She will have been surprised by Miheer. **Passive voice**

Imperative Sentences

What are imperative sentences?

Imperative sentences are used to express commands/orders or requests and also to give instructions or some advice. Imperative sentences do not require a subject. Furthermore, remember that the verb used in an imperative sentence should always be in the simple present tense. Imperative sentences end with a full stop or an exclamation mark.

Now, look at the following definitions to understand what imperative sentences are.

Definition of an Imperative Sentence

According to the Oxford Learner's Dictionary, an imperative sentence is defined as one "expressing an order" and according to the Cambridge Dictionary, an imperative sentence is "a sentence that gives a command or gives a request to do something". An imperative sentence, according to the Collins Dictionary, is one that is used to denote "a mood of verbs used in giving orders, making requests, etc." The Merriam-Webster Dictionary defines an imperative sentence as one that has the "power to restrain, control, and direct."

Types of Imperative Sentences with Examples

Imperative sentences can be divided into two main categories according to their nature namely,

- Positive imperative sentence
- Negative imperative sentence

Positive Imperative Sentence

A positive imperative sentence asks one to do something.

For example:

- Close the door.
- Call me when you get back.
- Wash the plates before you use them.

Negative Imperative Sentence

A negative imperative sentence is meant to do just the opposite. A negative imperative sentence instructs one not to do something.

For example:

- Do not close the door.
- Do not call me when you get back.
- Do not wash the plates before you use them.

Conditional Imperative Sentences

Another type of imperative sentences is the conditional imperative sentence. These sentences include a conditional clause and are mostly in the form of complex sentences.

For example:

- If you think you are going to be late, ask your brother to drop you off.
- When you get home, call me.
- Unless you want to go through all of it again, don't do it.

Uses of Imperative Sentences

Imperative sentences can be used in a variety of ways if you learn how to do it. Also, remember that just the imperative verb alone can pass as an imperative sentence.

For example:

- Go!
- Quiet!
- Run!

Now, let us look at some of the uses of imperative sentences that also categorises them into the different types. Imperative sentences can be used to do the following.

- To make a request
- To give a command
- To lend an invitation
- To give an instruction

Examples of Imperative Sentences

Given below are examples of imperative sentences that will definitely help you understand the topic better.

Making a request

- Please help me with this.
- Please pass the salt and pepper.
- Please reserve a seat for me.

Giving a command

- Don't leave the door open.
- Come home before sunset.
- Finish the assignment by tomorrow.

Leading an invitation

- Kindly join us for lunch after the reception.
- Come with me for a movie.
- Let us go for a walk.

Giving an instruction

- Sauté the onions until they turn golden brown.
- Boil the milk for at least two to three minutes.
- Stop when you see the red light.

Changing an imperative sentence in the active voice to passive voice

An imperative sentence in the passive voice has the following form: **Let + object + be + past participle.**

- Active: Carry it home.
  Passive: Let it be carried home.
- Active: Do it at once.
  Passive: Let it be done at once.
- Active: Open the door.
  Passive: Let the door be opened.
- Active: Throw the ball.
  Passive: Let the ball be thrown.

When the active voice is in the negative, the passive voice takes the form: **Let + object + not + be + past participle.**

- Active: Do not beat the dog.
  Passive: Let the dog not be beaten.

Note that **do** is not used in the passive form.
We can begin the passive sentence with **you** if we want to put emphasis on the person addressed to.

Compare:

- Active: Help me.
  Passive: Let me be helped.
  Passive: You are requested to help me.

- Active: Learn the poem.
  Passive: Let the poem be learned.
  Passive: You are asked to learn the poem.

- Active: Don't touch it.
  Passive: Let it not be touched.
  Passive: You are warned not to touch it.

Note that the passive form has to begin with **you** when the object of the active verb is not mentioned.

- Active: Work hard.

Here the active verb does not have an object. Therefore, the passive form should begin with **you.**

- Passive: You are advised to work hard.

- Active: Get out.
  Passive: You are ordered to get out.

Passive Voice Rules for Modals

The two basic rules for converting active voice into passive voice are as follows:

1. The places of subject and the object in a sentence are interchanged for converting active voice to passive voice.
2. Only the 3rd form of a verb (e.g., eaten) is as a main verb in passive voice.

Usage of auxiliary verbs in passive voice for Present, Future and Past Modals is explained is explained in the following tables.

Passive voices for Present & Future Modals
(e.8. CAN, SHOULD, MUST, MAY, MIGHT, OUGHT TO)

Present And Future Modals

(CAN, MUST, SHOULD, MAY, MIGHT,OUGHT)

Auxillary verb **be** is used with these modals in passive voice.

Active Voice	Passive Voice
CAN	**CAN BE**
He can drive a car.	A car can be driven by him.
He cannot drive a car.	A car cannot be driven by him.
Can he drive a car?	Can a car be driven by him?
He can make a chair.	A chair can be made by him.
He cannot make a chair.	A chair cannot be made by him.
Can he make a chair?	Can a chair be made by him?
MUST	**MUST BE**
He must return the loan.	The loan must be returned by him.
He must not return the loan.	The loan must not be returned by him.
Must he return the loan?	Must the loan be returned by him?
He must study this book.	This book must be studied by him.
He must not study this book.	This book must not be studied by him.
Must he study this book?	Must this book be studied by him?
MAY	**MAY BE**
I may eat an apple.	An apple may be eaten by me.

I may not eat an apple.	An apple may not be eaten by me.
May l eat an apple	May an apple be eaten by me?
He may buy a car.	A car may be bought by him.
He may not buy a car.	A car may not be bought by him.
May he buy a car?	May a car be bought by him.
SHOULD	**SHOULD BE**
I should buy this clock.	This cock should be bought by me.
I should not buy this clock.	This cock should not be bought by me.
Should I buy this clock?	Should this clock be bought by me?
MIGHT	**MIGHT BE**
He might win a prize.	A prize might be won by him.
He might not win a prize.	A prize might not be won by him.
Might he win a prize?	Might a prize be won by him?
She might finish the task.	The task might be finished by her.
She might not finish the task.	The task might not be finished by her.
Might she finish the task?	Might the task be finished by her.
OUGHT TO	**OUGHT TO BE**
You ought to clean this room.	The kid ought to be helped by him.

You ought not to clean this room.	Thot to be cleaned by
He ought to help the kid.	be cleaned by you.

Past Modals
(MIGHT HAVE, MAY HAVE, SHOULD HAVE, OUGHT HAVE, MUST HAVE)

Ausiliary verb "been" is used with these moda bs in Passive Voice.

Active Voice	Passive Voice
SHOULD HAPE	**SHOULD HAYE BEEN**
I should have started a job.	A job should have been started by me.
I should have not started a jab.	A job should not have been started by me.
Should I have started a job?	Should a jab have been started by me?
They should have helped the boy.	The boy should have been helped by them
They should have not he ped the boy.	The boy should not have been halped by them.
Should the have helped the boy?	Should the boy have been helped by them?
MUST HAVE	**MUST HAVE BEEN**
He must have paid the money.	The money must have been paid by him.
He must have not paid the money.	The money must not have been paid by him.
MAYHAVE	**MAY HAVE BEEN**
She may have eaten the meal.	The meal may have been eaten by her.
She may not have eaten the meal.	The meal may not have been eaten by her.

MIGHT HAVE	MIGHT HAVE QEEN
He might have eniayed the party.	The party might have been erioyed by him.
He might not have enioyed the party.	The party might not have been erioyed by him.
She might have passed the exam.	The exam might have been passed by her.
She might not have passed the exam	The exam might not have been passed by her.
OUGHT TO HAVE	**OUGHT TO HAVE BEEN**
You ought to have spoken the truth.	The truth ought to have been spaken by you.
You ought not to have told a lie.	A lie ought not to have been told by you.

MULTIPLE CHOICE QUESTION

Direction:

Select the option that expresses the given sentence in active voice and passive voice

1. Shut the door.

A. The door be shut

B. Shut the door

C. Let the door be shut

D. The door is shut

Answer: C

Explanation:

Let the door be shut

2. All the examinees have answered one particular question in the long answer writing section.

A. All the examinees answered one particular question in the long answer writing section

B. One particular question is answered by all the examinees in the long answer writing section

C. One particular question was answered by all the examinees in the long answer writing section

D. One particular question has been answered by all the examinees in the long answer writing section

Answer: D

Explanation:

The given sentence is of present perfect tense and it is in active form.

The structures for active/passive voices are:

Active: Subject + has/have + verb IIIrd form + object...

Passive: Object + has/have + been + verb IIIrd form + by + subject...

3. The members of the parliament elect their group leader either by consensus or by voice vote.

A. The group leader has been elected by the members of the parliament either by consensus or by voice vote

B. The group leader is elected by the members of the parliament either by consensus or by voice vote

C. The group leader was elected by the members of the parliament either by consensus or by voice vote

D. The members of the parliament are elected by their group leader either by consensus or by voice vote

Answer: B

Explanation:

Basic rules to be followed for Active/Passive conversions are:

Active: Subject + verb "s" or "es" with singular noun + object…

Passive: Object + Is/are/am + verb IIIrd form + by + subject…

4. The writer who passed away recently has authored a dozen novels and a number of poetry collections.

A. A dozen novels and a number of poetry collections were authored by the writer who passed away recently

B. A dozen novels and a number of poetry collections have been authored by the writer who passed away recently

C. A dozen novels and a number of poetry collections has been authored by the writer who passed away recently

D. A dozen novels and a number of poetry collections had been authored by the writer who passed away recently

Answer: B

Explanation:

The given sentence is of present perfect tense and it is in active form.

The structures for active/passive voices are:

Active: Subject + has/have + verb IIIrd form + object...

Passive: Object + has/have + been + verb IIIrd form + by + subject...

5. India won freedom with the blood and sweat of hundreds and thousands of Indians.

A. Freedom was won by India with the blood and sweat of hundreds and thousands of Indians

B. India had won freedom with the blood and sweat of hundreds and thousands of Indians

C. Freedom had been won by India with the blood and sweat of hundreds and thousands of Indians

D. Freedom was won by hundreds and thousands of Indians with their blood and sweat

Answer: A

Explanation:

The given sentence is in active form of simple past tense. The structures for active/passive voices are:
Active: Subject + verb IInd form + object...
Passive: Object + was/were + verb IIIrd form + by + subject...

6. They will have completed the work by the time we get there.
A. The work will have been completed by the time we get there.
B. The work will have been completed by the time we have got there.
C. The work will be completed by the time we get there.
D. The work will have completed by the time we get there.

Answer: A
Explanation:
"The work will have been completed by the time we get there" is the passive form for the sentence "
They will have completed the work by the time we get there
"By them" may be skipped because it is the completion of the work that is important than the subject "they".

7. The little boy asked the man the way to Athens.
A. The man was asked the way to Athens by the little boy.
B. The way to Athens was asked by the man from the little boy.
C. The man has been asked the way to Athens by the little boy.
D. The man was being asked the way to Athens by the little boy.

Answer: A
Explanation:
The given sentence is in past indefinite tense and conversion rule for changing passive to active voice is:
Active voice: Subject +V2 + object.
Passive voice: Subject + was/were +by +object.
Interchange the subject 'the little boy' into object and object 'The man' in subject accordingly to the rule.

8. Why did she break the garden wall ?
A. Why had the garden wall been broken by her ?
B. Why will the garden wall be broken by her ?
C. Why the garden wall was broken by her?
D. Why was the garden wall broken by her?

Answer: D
Explanation:
Why was the garden wall broken by her?

9. You should not offer meat to vegetarians.
A. Meat should be offered to non-vegetarians.
B. You should offer no meat to non-vegetarians.
C. Vegetarians should not be offered meat.
D. Vegetarians should not offer meat.

Answer: C
Explanation:
The given sentence is of active voice, and it uses a modal verb. The structures for active/passive voices for modal verbs are:
Active: Subject + modal verb + verb (Ist form) + object...
Passive: Object + modal verb + be + verb (IIIrd form) + by + subject...

10. You will be taken care of by me.
A. I would take care of you.
B. I will being take care of you.
C. I will be taking care of you.
D. I will take care of you.

Answer: D
Explanation:
I will take care of you. (Active) The sentence is in Simple Future Tense. (Passive)

11. People are raising a hue and cry and are breaking the furniture.
A. A hue and cry is being raised and the furniture are being broken by the people.
B. A hue and cry has been raised and the furniture has been broke.
C. A hue and cry is being raised and the furniture is being broken by the people.
D. Hue and cry and the furniture is being broken.

Answer: C
Explanation:
The given sentence is in present continues tense and conversion rule for changing activc to passive voice is
Active voice: Subject + is/am/are+ V1 + ing + object.
Passive voice: Subject + is/am/are + being + V3 + object.

12. One cannot expect children to understand these problems.
A. Children to understand these problems cannot be expected.
B. To understand these problems cannot be expected from children by one.
C. Children cannot be expected to understand these problems.
D. Children cannot be expected to be understood these problems.

Answer: C
Explanation:
Passive: Object + modal verb + not + be + verb (IInd form) + by + subject...

13. Ads on TV increase the sale of any commodity.
A. The sale of any commodity are increased by ads on TV.
B. The sale of any commodity is increased by ads on TV.
C. The sale of any commodity is being increased by ads on TV.
D. The sale of any commodity are being increased by ads on TV.

Answer: B
Explanation:
Active form: Sub + V1 + s/es + obj
Passive form: Obj + is/am/are + V3 + by + sub

14. We must respect the elders.
A. The elders must be respected.
B. Respect the elders we must.
C. The elders deserve respect from us.
D. The elders must respected by us.

Answer: A
Explanation:
The given sentence contains one of Model verb (Model Verb = will, shall, can, may, might, could, might, must, would). It is in active voice.

15. You will be looked after well.
A. They can't look after you well.
B. They shall look after you well.
C. They will look after you well.
D. They may look after well.

Answer: C
Explanation:
The given sentence is in passive voice of simple future tense. Let us understand the structures for active/passive voices for such sentences.
Active: Subject + will/shall + verb (Ist form) + object...
Passive: Object+ will/shall + be + verb (IIIrd form) + by + subject...

16. Have the box broken.
A. They have broken the box.
B. Get someone to break the box.
C. Have the broken box.
D. Break the box.

Answer: D
Explanation:
Break the box.

17. Do you imitate others?
A. Have others been imitated by you?
B. Were others being imitated by you?
C. Are others imitated by you?
D. Are others being imitated by you?

Answer: C
Explanation:
The given sentence is in Active voice. Use of 'being' is incorrect as no continuous action is described.

18. Did the noise frighten you?
A. Were you frighten by the noise?
B. Were you frightened by the noise?
C. Did you frighten the noise?
D. Was the noise frightened by you?

Answer: B
Explanation:
Were you frightened by the noise?

19. You must look into this matter.
A. This matter into looked by you.
B. This matter should be looked into by you.
C. This matter has been looked into by you.
D. This matter may be looked into by you.

Answer: B
Explanation:
The given sentence is in Active voice. The 'must' in the given sentence makes use of 'should be' necessary.

20. Darjeeling grows tea.
A. Tea is being grown in Darjeeling.
B. Let the tea be grown in Darjeeling.
C. Tea grows in Darjeeling.
D. Tea is grown in Darjeeling.

Answer: D
Explanation:
Tea is grown in Darjeeling.

21. The storm did much damage.
A. The storm was damaged.
B. Much damage did the storm.
C. Much damage was done by the storm.
D. The storm damaged much.

Answer: C
Explanation:
Much damage was done by the storm.

22. We are reaching the end of this exercise.
A. The exercise has reached its end by us.
B. This is our end to the exercise.
C. This exercise is ended by us.
D. The end of this exercise is being reached by us.

Answer: D
Explanation:

The given sentence is in Active voice. Note that the word 'reach' should be used when re-writing the sentence in Passive voice.

23. I expect you to complete this work before sunset.
A. You are expected to be completed this work before sunset.
B. You are expected to complete this work before sunset.
C. I expect you to be completed this work before sunset.
D. I am expected to complete this work before sunset.

Answer: B
Explanation:
You are expected to complete this work before sunset.

24. It is time to take tea.
A. It is time that tea had been taken.
B. It is time that tea should be taken.
C. It was time that tea was taken.
D. It is time for tea to be taken.

Answer: D
Explanation:
It is time for tea to be taken.

25. Why did you not agree to my proposal?
A. Why was my proposal not agreed to by you?
B. Why my proposal was not agreed to by you?
C. Why was my proposal not agreed to?
D. Why was my proposal not agreed by you?

Answer: A
Explanation:
Why was my proposal not agreed to by you?

26. Her mother bought the house.
A. The house will be bought by her mother.
B. The house had been bought by her mother.
C. The house was being bought by her mother.
D. The house was bought by her mother.

Answer: D
Explanation:
The house was bought by her mother.

27. Do not disturb the patient.
A. The patient will not be disturbed.
B. The patient is not to be disturbed.
C. Let the patient not be disturbed.
D. The patient should not be disturbed.

Answer: B
Explanation:
The patient is not to be disturbed.

28. I saw him leaving the house.
A. He was seen leaving the house by me.
B. Leaving the house he was seen by me.
C. He had been seen leaving the house.
D. He was seen to be leaving the house.

Answer: A
Explanation:
He was seen leaving the house by me.

29. Sheeba posted a letter.
A. Sheeba was being posted by a letter.
B. A letter has been posted by Sheeba.
C. A letter was posted by Sheeba.
D. A letter was being posted by Sheeba.

Answer: C
Explanation:
The given sentence is in Active voice. Note that the tense of the verb in the given sentence should not be changed while changing the voice of the sentence.

30. A lion may be helped even by a little mouse.
A. Even a little mouse ought to help a lion.
B. A little mouse can even help a lion.
C. A little mouse may even help a lion.

D. Even a little mouse may help a lion.

Answer: D
Explanation:
Even a little mouse may help a lion.

31. Our task had been completed before sunset.
A. We completed our task before sunset.
B. We have completed our task before sunset.
C. We complete our task before sunset.
D. We had completed our task before sunset.

Answer: D
Explanation:
The given sentence is in passive voice and it is in Past Perfect Tense.
To convert it into active voice, we just remove been from the given sentence and object ourwill be change into subject We.
Rule : Subject + had + V3 + Other agents.

32. The boy laughed at the beggar.
A. The beggar was laughed by the boy.
B. The beggar was being laughed by the boy.
C. The beggar was being laughed at by the boy.
D. The beggar was laughed at by the boy.

Answer: D
Explanation:
Given sentence is in Past indefinite Past simple tense and it is in the active voice. To change it into Passive voice Object the boy will become subject and subject The beggar will be object. We also use helping verb of past simple tense was with V3 form of the main verb. Keep it in mind that the preposition at must be retained with the verb.
Rule :
Subject + was /were + V3 + Other Agents.

33. The boys were paying cricket.
A. Cricket had been played by the boys.
B. Cricket has been played by the boys.
C. Cricket was played by the boys.
D. Cricket was being played by the boys.

Answer: D

Explanation:

The given sentence is in Past Continuous Tense and it is in active voice. We need to change it into Passive voice.

Rule :

Subject + was /were + being + V3 + Optional Agents.

34. They drew a circle in the morning.

A. A circle was being drawn by them in the morning.

B. A circle was drawn by them in the morning.

C. In the morning a circle have been drawn by them.

D. A circle has been drawing since morning.

Answer: B

Explanation:

Given sentence is in Past simple tense and it is in active voice, we need to change it into passive voice.

Rule : Subject + was / were + V3 + Optional Agents.

35. They will demolish the entire block.

A. The entire block is being demolished.

B. The block may be demolished entirely.

C. The entire block will have to be demolished by them.

D. The entire block will be demolished.

Answer: D

Explanation:

The given sentence contains one of Model verb Model Verb = will, shall, can, may, might, could, might, must, would. It is in active voice.

Rule : Subject + Model verb + be + V3 + Optional Objects.

Direction:

Select the option that expresses the given sentence in passive voice.

36. Mandeep has repaired the truck.

A. The truck have been repaired by Mandeep.

B. The truck had been repaired by Mandeep.

C. The truck is been repaired by Mandeep.

D. The truck has been repaired by Mandeep.

Answer: D

Explanation:

- The given sentence is in the present perfect tense.
- Passive Voice sentences of Present Perfect Tense use “has/have” along with “been” as a helping verb with respective number nouns and pronouns.
- Sentence structure:
- Active: Subject + has/have + V3 + object.
- Passive: Object + has/have + been + V3 + by + subject.

Direction:

A sentence has been given in Active/Passive voice. Out of the four alternatives suggested, select the one which best expresses the same sentence in Passive/Active voice.

37. The government has to take necessary precautions against this new virus to protect people from getting infected.

A. Necessary precautions are being taken by the government against this new virus to protect the people from getting infected.

B. Necessary precautions should have been taken by the government against this new virus to protect the people from getting infected.

C. Necessary precautions have been taken by the government against this new virus to protect the people from getting infected.

D. Necessary precautions have to be taken by the government against this new virus to protect people from getting infected.

Answer: D

Explanation:

- In Active Voice, a sentence emphasizes the subject, performing an action.
- In Passive Voice, a sentence emphasizes the action or the object of the sentence.
- The given sentence is in the active voice and 'The government' is the subject and "necessary precautions" is the object.
- When we convert this sentence into passive voice, the subject 'The government' of the active voice becomes the object, the object "necessary precautions" becomes the subject.
- The singular verb 'has' becomes plural 'have' for the plural subject 'precautions'.
- The passive format "be + V3 (taken)" should be used.
- This is the active and passive voice rule for the present simple tense.

Direction:

A sentence has been given in Active/Passive Voice. Out of the four alternatives suggested, select the one which best expresses the same sentence in Passive/Active Voice.

38. By that time, Vikash Ranjan was elected Mayor of the city by the people for three times.

A. By that time, the people have elected Vikash Ranjan Mayor of the city for three times.

B. By that time, the people had elected Vikash Ranjan Mayor of the city for three times.

C. By that time, the people elected Vikash Ranjan Mayor of the city for three times.

D. By that time, the people were elected Mayor by Vikash Ranjan for three times.

Answer: C

Explanation:

- The 'voice' of a verb tells us whether the subject of the sentence performs or receives the action.
- The given sentence is in the passive voice.
- While changing a sentence from passive voice to active voice, the object and subject are interchanged with each other, i.e. object of the passive sentence becomes the subject of the active sentence and vice versa. Their cases also change accordingly.

Direction:

Out of the given options, choose the one which is the correct passive voice of the sentence given below.

39. I had not completed the assignment.

A. The assignment have not been completed by me.

B. The assignment were not being completed by me

C. The assignment were not completed by me.

D. The assignment had not been completed by me.

Answer: D

Explanation:

- The above question given in active voice we have to change it into the passive voice.
- The above sentence is an example of the past perfect tense.
- The structure of these kinds of sentence is :-
  - ❖ Sub. + had + V3 + by + Obj.(active form). Example: I had done my homework
  - ❖ Sub. (objective case) + had + been + v3 + by + Object.(subjective case). Example: My homework had been done by me.

Direction:

Select the correct active form of the given sentence.

40. Perfection is sought by him in everything he does.

A. He is seeking perfection in everything he does.

B. He has sought perfection in everything he does.

C. He sought perfection in everything he did.

D. He seeks perfection in everything he does.

Answer: D

Explanation:

- In Active Voice, a sentence emphasizes the subject, performing an action.
- In Passive Voice, a sentence emphasizes the action or the object of the sentence.
- The given sentence is in the passive voice and 'Perfection' is the subject and 'him' is the object.
- When we convert this sentence into active voice, the subject 'Perfection' of the active voice becomes the object, the object 'him' becomes the subject 'he'.
- The passive format "is + V3 (sought)" should be converted into the active format "V1 (seeks)".
- This is the active and passive voice rule for the present simple tense.

Direction:

Select the correct active form of the given sentence.

41. The migrant was bidden to leave the country by the authority.

A. The authority bid the migrant to leave the country.

B. The authority bade the migrant leave the country.

C. Let the migrant bade to leave the country.

D. The authority bade the migrant to leave the country.

Answer: B

Explanation:

- Find the subject and object of the sentence and exchange their places; make changes in their cases as well if subject and object are pronouns.
- Here the question is given in Passive Voice so it has to be changed into Active Voice.
- If the verbs like Let, bid, help, and make are used in Active Voice followed by a Bare Infinitive and if they are used in Passive Voice then they are followed by Infinitive, not Bare Infinitive.

Direction:

Select the option that expresses the given sentence in active voice.

42. The hunchback was being laughed at by everyone

A. Everyone is laughing at the hunchback

B. Everyone laughs at the hunchback

C. Everyone laughed at the hunchback.

D. Everyone was laughing at the hunchback.

Answer: D

Explanation:

- In Active Voice, a sentence emphasizes subject performing an action.
- In Passive Voice, a sentence emphasizes the action or the object of the sentence.
- The given sentence is in the passive voice and 'The hunchback' is the subject and 'everyone' is the object.
- When we convert this sentence into active voice, the subject 'The hunchback' of the passive voice becomes the object, the object 'everyone' becomes the subject.
- The passive format "was + being + V3" is used and the active format "was + ing" should be used.
- This is the active and passive voice rule for the past continuous tense.
- Hence, "Everyone was laughing at the hunchback" is the correct active voice.

Direction:

Select the option that expresses the given sentence in passive voice.

43. Give the child a nourishing diet.

A. The child should be given a nourishing diet.

B. The child was given a nourishing diet.

C. The child must have given a nourishing diet.

D. The child is given a nourishing diet

Answer: A

Explanation:

- The given sentence is in the Active Voice. As per the given question we have to change the sentence into Passive Form.
- The transformation of these kinds of sentences is:
  - ❖ The given sentence is an example of an imperative sentence.
  - ❖ The notion of the given sentence is the suggestion.
  - ❖ V1 + Object. (Active Voice)
  - ❖ Subject (Objective case) + should + be + V3. (Passive Voice)

Direction:

Select the correct passive form of the given sentence.

44. They have invited the parents as well as the child.

A. The parents as well as the child has been invited.

B. The parents as well as the child have been invited.

C. The child as well as the parents has been invited.

D. The parents as well as the child had been invited by them.

Answer: B

Explanation:

- The instructions given below should be followed while changing an assertive sentence to passive voice.
- Find the subject and object of the sentence and exchange their places; make changes in their cases as well if subject and object are pronouns.
- Use preposition by before the agent.
- Use an appropriate helping verb in passive form according to the tense of the active form. (Present perfect - has/have + been)
- Always use the third form of the main verb in passive form.
- At last line up the remaining part.

Direction:

A sentence is given in Active/Passive voice. Out of the four alternatives suggested, select the one which best expresses the same sentence in Active/Passive voice.

45. Rahul is playing cricket in the playground provided by the government.

A. Cricket is played by Rahul in the playground provided by the government.

B. Cricket has been played by Rahul in the playground provided by the government.

C. Cricket is been played by Rahul in the playground provided by the government.

D. Cricket is being played by Rahul in the playground provided by the government.

Answer: D

Explanation:

Whenever a sentence in present continuous tense is changed into its passive voice, then we follow the given structure:-

'Is/am/are + Ving' is changed to 'is/am/are + being + V3'.

Direction:

Choose the correct Passive Construction for the sentence given:

46. "Mrs. Sharma knows me."

A. I am known by Mrs. Sharma.
B. I was known by Mrs. Sharma.
C. I am known to Mrs. Sharma.
D. I have known to Mrs. Sharma

Answer: C
Explanation:

- In the Active Voice, the emphasis is on the subject which performs an action.
- In the Passive Voice, the emphasis is on the object of the sentence which is the receiver or recipient of the action being performed.
- In the given sentence, the subject is 'Mrs. Sharma' and the object is 'me'.
- The sentence is in the present indefinite tense.
- The structure is:
- Sub + V1 (s/es) + object.
- In the passive voice, the structure is:
- Obj + is/am/are + the past particple (V3) + (by + subject).
- We use the preposition 'to' after 'known'. So, we won't use 'by' here.

Direction:
Select the correct passive form of the given sentence.
47. The police beat a number of protestors last night.
A. A number of protestors had been beaten by the police last night.
B. A number of protestors were being beaten by the police last night.
C. A number of protestors has been beaten by the police the night before.
D. A number of protestors were beaten by the police last night.

Answer: D
Explanation:

- In Active Voice, a sentence emphasizes the subject, performing an action.
- In Passive Voice, a sentence emphasizes the action or the object of the sentence.
- The given sentence is in the active voice and 'The police' is the subject and 'a number of protestors' is the object.
- When we convert this sentence into passive voice, the subject 'The police' of the active voice becomes the object, the object 'a number of protestors' becomes the subject.
- The passive format "were + V3" should be used.
- This is the active and passive voice rule for the past simple tense.

Direction:

Change the given sentence into passive voice.

48. Whom did you laugh at?

A. By whom was you laughed at?

B. Who was laughed at by you?

C. you were laughed at by whom?

D. Did you laugh at who?

Answer: B

Explanation:

- The given sentence is in Active Voice. As per the given question we have to change it into Passive Voice.
- Here, in the given sentence the direct object 'whom' in the active sentence will become the subject in the passive sentence, and its form is 'who'.
- Hence, 'whom' will be changed into 'who'.
- 'did laugh' will be changed into 'was laughed'.
- Lastly, the 'by' preposition will be added.

Direction:

Select the option that expresses the given sentence in passive voice.

49. She handles all tasks efficiently.

A. All tasks are handled efficiently by her.

B. All tasks were handled efficiently by her.

C. All tasks have been handled efficiently by her.

D. All tasks are being handled efficiently by her.

Answer: A

Explanation:

- The given sentence is in Active Voice. As per the question we have to change it into Passive Voice.
- The structure of the given sentence is as follows:
  - ❖ Subject + V1 + Object. (Active Voice)
  - ❖ Subject (Objective Case) + is/am/are + V3 + Object (Subjective Case). (Passive Voice)

Direction:

A sentence is given in Active/Passive voice. Out of the four alternatives suggested, select the one which best expresses the same sentence in Active/Passive voice.

50. His scores in the matches surprised me.
A. I was surprised by his scores in the matches.
B. I was surprised at his scores in the matches.
C. I was surprised on his scores in the matches.
D. I was surprised to his scores in the matches.

Answer: B
Explanation:

- In the above given sentence, the correct passive form of the given sentence will be 'I was surprised at his scores in the matches'.
- I t is so because some verbs are used with fixed prepositions in the passive form as well.
- Words like surprised and disappointed are always used with a fixed preposition i.e. 'at' or 'with'
- For Example:-
  - ❖ Active Voice - His marks surprised me.
  - ❖ Passive Voice - I was surprised at his marks.

Introduction

A cloze test is a language proficiency assessment technique in which words are omitted from a text and replaced with blanks. The purpose of a cloze test is to evaluate the reader's understanding of the language, ability to comprehend the text, and to fill in the missing words with correct vocabulary, grammar, and syntax. The words that are left out of the text can be chosen randomly or strategically, depending on the purpose of the test. A cloze test is often used in language learning and teaching to assess a learner's language proficiency or in other fields such as psychology or linguistics to assess cognitive and linguistic abilities.

A Cloze test is a sentence completion test. Candidates are required to make a choice from multiple alternatives for each word blanked out, not in a sentence but in the passage. Such types of questions are asked to check the candidate's vocabulary power and the ability to understand the passage as a whole is assessed. Mainly 4-8 questions are asked from the cloze test topic in the exams, especially SSC, Bank, Insurance, and RRB exams. Candidates can score good marks easily in this section with sound reading aptitude.

There Are Different Types of Cloze Tests, Including

1. **Deletion Cloze Test:** This type of cloze test involves deleting every nth word from a text, leaving blank spaces for the test taker to fill in the missing words.

2. **Syntax Cloze Test:** This type of cloze test requires test takers to fill in the blanks with the appropriate grammatical form of the missing word.

3. **Discourse Cloze Test:** This type of cloze test requires test takers to use their understanding of the context and coherence of a passage to fill in the blanks.

4. **Sentence Completion Cloze Test:** This type of cloze test involves providing a sentence with a missing word or phrase, and the test taker must fill in the blank with the correct answer.

5. **Picture Cloze Test:** In this type of cloze test, a picture or diagram is presented, and test takers must fill in the missing words or phrases that relate to the image.

6. **Open-Ended Cloze Test:** This type of cloze test allows test takers to provide any word or phrase they think is appropriate to fill in the blank spaces, without being restricted by specific options.

Some Terms Commonly Used in Cloze Tests Include

1. **Cloze Passage:** The passage of text that contains blanks or omissions, which the test taker must fill in.

2. **Target Words:** The words that have been removed from the cloze passage and need to be filled in by the test taker.

3. **Deletion Ratio:** The percentage of words that have been deleted from the cloze passage to create the test.

4. **Context:** The surrounding words or phrases in the cloze passage that provide clues to the test taker about what word or phrase should be used to fill in the blank.

5. **Validity:** The extent to which the cloze test measures what it is supposed to measure and is an accurate representation of the test taker's language proficiency.

6. **Reliability:** The consistency and stability of the cloze test over time and across different test takers, indicating the test's ability to yield consistent results.

7. **Scoring:** The method used to evaluate the test taker's responses, whether they are scored based on the accuracy of the answer or the quality of the response.

Cloze Tests Have Several Uses, Including

1. **Language Proficiency Assessment:** Cloze tests are commonly used in language learning and teaching to assess a learner's language proficiency, particularly their reading comprehension skills.

2. **Academic Research:** Cloze tests are also used in academic research in fields such as linguistics and psychology to investigate cognitive and linguistic processes, including language processing, memory, and attention.

3. **Job Screening:** Cloze tests can be used in job screening processes to assess a candidate's language proficiency and suitability for a specific job that requires strong language skills.

4. **Educational Diagnosis:** Cloze tests can be used to diagnose a student's language weaknesses and strengths, which can help teachers tailor their teaching to meet the individual needs of their students.

5. **Curriculum Design:** Cloze tests can be used in curriculum design to help teachers develop appropriate language materials for their students and to assess the effectiveness of their teaching strategies.

6. **Standardized Testing:** Cloze tests can be used as part of standardized language tests to measure the language proficiency of a large population, such as in national or international language proficiency tests.

Here Are Some General Rules for Cloze Tests

1. Read the entire passage carefully to understand the context and meaning.
2. Pay attention to the sentence structure and grammar to help determine the missing words.
3. Look for contextual clues, such as synonyms or antonyms, to help fill in the missing words.
4. Use your prior knowledge of the topic to help you fill in the missing words.
5. Use process of elimination to eliminate options that do not fit in the context.
6. Try to maintain consistency of tense, voice, and person while filling in the blanks.

7. Check your spelling and punctuation before submitting your answers.
8. Follow the instructions carefully, including the deletion ratio, scoring system, and time limit.
9. Use any provided feedback to understand your strengths and weaknesses and to improve your language skills.
10. Practice regularly to improve your language proficiency and your ability to fill in the missing words accurately and efficiently.

Merits

1. **Assess Multiple Skills:** Cloze tests can assess multiple language skills, such as vocabulary, grammar, reading comprehension, and context-dependent meaning.

2. **Objective and Reliable:** Cloze tests are objective and reliable, as the same test can be given to different test takers, and the same scoring criteria can be applied to all.

3. **Contextualized:** Cloze tests are contextualized, as they use real-life or realistic scenarios to assess a test taker's understanding of language, making the test more relevant and meaningful.

4. **Time Efficient:** Cloze tests can be completed in a short period of time, making them a quick and efficient way to assess a test taker's language proficiency.

5. **Flexible:** Cloze tests can be adapted to suit different language proficiency levels and test purposes by varying the deletion ratio, text complexity, and scoring criteria.

Demerits

1. **Limited Assessment:** Cloze tests may not fully capture a test taker's language proficiency, as they only assess a limited set of language skills and may not be able to assess oral proficiency or communicative ability.

2. **Context Dependency:** Cloze tests are context-dependent, and test takers may be able to answer questions correctly based on contextual clues rather than their actual understanding of the language.

3. **Limited Feedback:** Cloze tests may provide limited feedback to test takers, as they only assess the test taker's response to the missing words and may not provide feedback on other aspects of language proficiency.

4. **Deletion Ratio Bias:** The deletion ratio used in cloze tests can bias the test towards certain language skills or aspects of language, which may not be representative of the test taker's overall language proficiency.
5. **Difficulty:** Cloze tests can be difficult, especially if the deletion ratio is high or if the text is complex, which can lead to test anxiety and affect test performance.

MULTIPLE CHOICE QUESTIONS

Direction:

The following questions, you have several passages where some of the words have been left out. Read the passages carefully and choose the correct answer to each blank out of the four alternatives

PASSAGE–I (Questions 1-10)

Childhood is a time when there are ___(1)___ responsibilities to make life difficult. If a child ___(2)___ good parents, he is fed, looked ___(3)___ and loved, whatever he may do. It is improbable that he will ever again in his life ___(4)___ given so much without having to do anything ___(5)___ return. In addition, life is always ___(6)___ new things to the child. A child finds ___(7)___ in playing in the rain or in the snow. His first visit ___(8)___ the seaside is a marvellous adventure. But a child has his pains; he is not so free to do as he wishes; he is continually being ___(9)___ not to do things or is being ___(10)___. His life is therefore not perfectly happy

1. Fill in the blank.

A. many

B. little

C. few

D. more

Answer: C

Explanation:

few (Det., Adj.)

2. Fill in the blank.

A. had

B. have

C. has

D. will have

Answer: C

Explanation:

has (Aux.V.)

3. Fill in the blank.

A. up

A. at

B. after

C. around

Answer: C

Explanation:

after (Prep.)

4. Fill in the blank.

A. is

B. has

C. are

D. be

Answer: D

Explanation:

be (Aux. V.)

5. Fill in the blank.

A. for

B. in

C. as

D. of

Answer: B

Explanation:

in (Prep.)

6. Fill in the blank.

A. donating

B. displaying

C. granting

D. presenting

Answer: D

Explanation:
presenting (Verb)

7. Fill in the blank.
A. pain
B. progress
C. pressure
D. pleasure

Answer: D
Explanation:
pleasure (Noun

8. Fill in the blank.
A. on
B. to
C. in
D. for

Answer: B
Explanation:
to (Prep.)

9. Fill in the blank.
A. ordered
B. told
C. forbidden
D. restricted

Answer: B
Explanation:
told (Verb)

10. Fill in the blank.
A. beaten
B. penalised

C. disturbed
D. punished

Answer: D
Explanation:
punished (Verb)

Direction:
In the following passage, some of the words have been left out. First read the passage over and try to understand what it is about. Then fill in the blanks with the help of the alternatives given.

PASSAGE–II (Question 11-20)
It was a sudden decision. Three of us, all ___(1)___ in the hostel, decided to travel by train to ___(2)___ and witness the Republic Day Parade. The station was heavily ___(3)___ and there was a long queue before the ticket counter. ___(4)___ pretended sickness and persuaded the man nearest to the ___(5)___ to buy three more tickets – one for him and ___(6)___ for his sisters. No problem, therefore, in buying tickets. ___(7)___ train was already at the platform and there was ___(8)___ mad rush among the passengers to get on the coaches. Hari would not be worried by ___(9)___. He asked ___(10)___ to jump over the bumper between two coaches to get on to the other side.

11. Choose the most appropriate word for blank.
A. roommates
B. strangers
C. classmates
D. friends

Answer: A
Explanation:
room-mates (Noun)

12. Choose the most appropriate word for blank.
A. Calcutta
B. Hyderabad
C. Chennai

D. Delhi

Answer: D
Explanation:
Delhi (Noun)

13. Choose the most appropriate word for blank.
A. guarded
B. thronged
C. crowded
D. filled

Answer: C
Explanation:
crowded (Adj.)

14. Choose the most appropriate word for blank.
A. She
B. Hari
C. They
D. You

Answer: B
Explanation:
Hari (Noun)

15. Choose the most appropriate word for blank.
A. door
B. window
C. counter
D. enhance

Answer: C
Explanation:
counter (Noun)

16. Choose the most appropriate word for blank.

A. three

B. four

C. one

D. two

Answer: D

Explanation:

two (Det.)

17. Choose the most appropriate word for blank.

A. The

B. A

C. An

D. No

Answer: A

Explanation:

the (Def. Art.)

18. Choose the most appropriate word for blank.

A. a

B. an

C. the

D. not

Answer: A

Explanation:

a (Indef. Art.)

19. Choose the most appropriate word for blank.

A. things

B. everything

C. anything

D. something

Answer: C

Explanation:

anything (Pro.)

20. Choose the most appropriate word for blank.

A. them

B. us

C. we

D. they

Answer: B

Explanation:

us (Pro.)

Direction:

In each of the following passages there are blanks, each of which has been indicated as A, B to E. Choose the correct word from the given options which fits the blank appropriately.

PASSAGE–III (Question 21-25)

When both myths and countermyths occur in the narrative field of a society, people can ___(A)___ the oppositions between them in unique ways. The psychological relevance of stories in the cases of myths and horror films may be in the experiencing of the ___(B)___ binary tensions, rather than in the manifest ___(C)___ of the story. The tensions in the story is, however, ___(D)___ through the binary contrasts. The message conveyed is a ___(E)___ complex.

21. Choose the exact word from the given below option.

A. internalize

B. externalize

C. concretize

D. secularize

Answer: A

Explanation:

internalize

22. Choose the exact word from the given below option.
A. overlying
B. destructive
C. comforting
D. underlying

Answer: D
Explanation:
underlying

23. Choose the exact word from the given below option.
A. relay
B. education
C. content
D. morality

Answer: C
Explanation:
content

24. Choose the exact word from the given below option.
A. dissolved
B. dissipated
C. opposed
D. maintained

Answer: D
Explanation:
maintained

25. Choose the exact word from the given below option.
A. holistic
B. constructive
C. difficult
D. prolific

Answer: A

Explanation:

Holistic

Direction:

The following questions, you have several passages where some of the words have been left out. Read the passages carefully and choose the correct answer to each blanks with its particular number, out of the five alternatives.

PASSAGE–IV (Question 26-35)

____(1)____stringent anti-pollution laws, mass awareness levels in India about the need to ____(2)____ the environment are low. Which is ____(3)____ many people insist that mere laws won't do; what we ____(4)____ need are "environment conscious" citizens. It is in this context that the University's ____(5)____ to introduce environment studies as a compulsory paper at the undergraduate level ____(6)____ significance. There was some ____(7)____ initially about who would teach the paper because financial ____(8)____ make it impossible for colleges to ____(9)____ approval for new teaching posts. In fact, in August 1999, the University Grants Commission (UGC) imposed a ban on the creation of new teaching posts in colleges. ____(10)____ with this problem, authorities at the university have decided that serving teachers belonging to various disciplines will teach the paper.₹

26. Identify the exact answer for the blank (1)?

A. Despite

B. Having

C. Enacting

D. Adopting

Answer: (a)

Explanation:

Despite

27. Identify the exact answer for the blank (2)?

A. contaminate

B. clean

C. filter

D. protect

Answer: (d)

Explanation:

protect

28. Identify the exact answer for the blank (3)?

A. resulting

B. why

C. obvious

D. as

Answer: (b)

Explanation:

why

29. Identify the exact answer for the blank (4)?

A. seldom

B. don't

C. hardly

D. actually

Answer: (d)

Explanation:

actually

30. Identify the exact answer for the blank (5)?

A. inability

B. deferral

C. decision

D. failure

Answer: (c)

Explanation:

decision

31. Identify the exact answer for the blank (6)?

A. extracts

B. accord
C. expects
D. assumes

Answer: (d)
Explanation:
assumes

32. Identify the exact answer for the blank (7)?
A. displeasure
B. antagonism
C. hurdles
D. confusion

Answer: (d)
Explanation:
confusion

33. Identify the exact answer for the blank (8)?
A. losses
B. constraints
C. apathy
D. soundness

Answer: (b)
Explanation:
constraints

34. Identify the exact answer for the blank (9)?
A. receive
B. establish
C. emphasize
D. expect

Answer: (a)
Explanation:

receive

35. Identify the exact answer for the blank (10)?

A. Down

B. Familiarity

C. Solution

D. Convinced

Answer: (c)

Explanation:

Solution

Direction:

In each of the following passages there are blanks, each of which has been indicated as A, B, C to J. Choose the correct word from the given options which fits the blank appropriately.

PASSAGE–V (Question 36-45)

There is an old story told of a man who ___(A)___ into a deep sleep, His friend stayed by him as long as he ___(B)___. Being compelled to go and fearing that he might be in want, the friend hid a ___(C)___ in the old man's garment, When the old man ___(D)___, not ___(E)___ that his friend had ___(F)___ a jewel in his garment, he wandered about in ___(G)___, hungry. A long time afterwards, the two men met again. The friend told the poor man about the jewel and ___(H)___ him to look for it. Like the old man in the story, people ___(I)___ about in this life, ___(J)___ of what is hidden away in their inner nature, pure and untarnished.

36. Fill the blanks with the help of alternatives given below.

A. fell

B. fall

C. slept

D. fallen

Answer: A

Explanation:

fell

37. Fill the blanks with the help of alternatives given below.
A. can
B. could
C. should
D. will

Answer: B
Explanation:
could

38. Fill the blanks with the help of alternatives given below.
A. sparkle
B. glimmer
C. jewel
D. treasure

Answer: C
Explanation:
jewel

39. Fill the blanks with the help of alternatives given below.
A. wake
B. waken
C. arise
D. awoke

Answer: D
Explanation:
awoke

40. Fill the blanks with the help of alternatives given below.
A. knowing
B. know
C. known
D. knew

Answer: A

Explanation:

Knowing

41. Fill the blanks with the help of alternatives given below.

A. hiding

B. hidden

C. conceal

D. hide

Answer: B

Explanation:

hidden

42. Fill the blanks with the help of alternatives given below.

A. vane

B. vein

C. vain

D. wane

Answer: C

Explanation:

vain

43. Fill the blanks with the help of alternatives given below.

A. propose

B. considered

C. suggested

D. advised

Answer: D

Explanation:

advised

44. Fill the blanks with the help of alternatives given below.

A. wander

B. wonder
C. direct
D. change
Answer: A
Explanation:
wander

45. Fill the blanks with the help of alternatives given below.
A. conscious
B. unconscious
C. aware
D. subconscious

Answer: B
Explanation:
Unconscious

Direction:
In the following passage, some words have been deleted. Fill in the blanks with the help of the alternatives given. Select the most appropriate option for each number.

PASSAGE–VI (Question 46–50)
Life is full of ___1___ types of experiences. Strange, in fact, are the ways of God. If a man is happy today, he may be __2____ unhappy the very next day. Some ___3___ are pleasant and joyful while others are full of ___4___ and pain. If at one time a person finds himself on top of the world, at the ___5___ time he is depressed and downcast.

46. Fill the blanks with the help of alternatives given below.
A. allied
B. amplified
C. varied
D. systematic

Answer: C
Explanation:
varied

47. Fill the blanks with the help of alternatives given below.
A. quite
B. major
C. most
D. quietly

Answer: A
Explanation:
quite

48. Fill the blanks with the help of alternatives given below.
A. customs
B. experiences
C. tenderizes
D. rituals

Answer: B
Explanation:
experiences

49. Fill the blanks with the help of alternatives given below.
A. echoes
B. pathos
C. ethos
D. mythos

Answer: B
Explanation:
pathos

50. Fill the blanks with the help of alternatives given below.
A. last
B. other
C. most
D. second

Answer: B
Explanation:
other

www.ingramcontent.com/pod-product-compliance
Ingram Content Group UK Ltd.
Pitfield, Milton Keynes, MK11 3LW, UK
UKHW061703190726
13853UKWH00008B/2373